Hands-on Matplotlib

Learn Plotting and Visualizations with Python 3

Ashwin Pajankar

Apress®

Hands-on Matplotlib

Ashwin Pajankar
Nashik, Maharashtra, India

ISBN-13 (pbk): 978-1-4842-7409-5   ISBN-13 (electronic): 978-1-4842-7410-1
https://doi.org/10.1007/978-1-4842-7410-1

Managing Director, Apress Media LLC: Welmoed Spahr
Acquisitions Editor: Celestin Suresh John
Development Editor: James Markham
Coordinating Editor: Aditee Mirashi

Cover designed by eStudioCalamar

Cover image designed by Freepik (www.freepik.com)

Distributed to the book trade worldwide by Springer Science+Business Media New York, 1 New York Plaza, Suite 4600, New York, NY 10004-1562, USA. Phone 1-800-SPRINGER, fax (201) 348-4505, e-mail orders-ny@springer-sbm.com, or visit www.springeronline.com. Apress Media, LLC is a California LLC and the sole member (owner) is Springer Science + Business Media Finance Inc (SSBM Finance Inc). SSBM Finance Inc is a **Delaware** corporation.

For information on translations, please e-mail booktranslations@springernature.com; for reprint, paperback, or audio rights, please e-mail bookpermissions@springernature.com.

Apress titles may be purchased in bulk for academic, corporate, or promotional use. eBook versions and licenses are also available for most titles. For more information, reference our Print and eBook Bulk Sales web page at www.apress.com/bulk-sales.

Any source code or other supplementary material referenced by the author in this book is available to readers on GitHub via the book's product page, located at www.apress.com/978-1-4842-7409-5. For more detailed information, please visit www.apress.com/source-code.

Printed on acid-free paper

This book is dedicated to the memory of my teacher,
Prof. Govindarajulu Regeti
(July 9, 1945, to March 18, 2021).

Popularly known to everyone as RGR, Prof. Govindarajulu obtained
his B.Tech in electrical and electronic engineering from JNTU
Kakinada. He also earned an M.Tech and a Ph.D. from IIT Kanpur.
Prof. Govindarajulu was an early faculty member of IIIT Hyderabad
and played a significant role in making IIIT Hyderabad the top-class
institution that it is today. He was by far the most loved and respected
faculty member of the institute. He was full of energy to teach and full
of old-fashioned charm. There is no doubt he cared for every student as
an individual, taking care to know about and to guide them.
He taught, guided, and mentored many batches of students at
IIIT Hyderabad (including the author of this book).

Table of Contents

About the Author

Ashwin Pajankar earned a Master of Technology in computer science engineering from IIIT Hyderabad and has more than 25 years of experience in the area of programming. He started his journey in programming and electronics at the tender age of 7 with the BASIC programming language and is now proficient in Assembly programming, C, C++, Java, shell scripting, and Python. His other technical expertise includes single-board computers such as the Raspberry Pi and Banana Pro, microcontroller boards such as the Arduino, and embedded boards such as the BBC Micro Bit.

He is currently a freelance online instructor teaching programming to more than 70,000 professionals. He also regularly conducts live programming bootcamps for software professionals. His growing YouTube channel has an audience of more than 10,000 subscribers. He has published more than 15 books on programming and electronics.

In addition to his technology work, he volunteers for many social causes. He has won several awards at his university and past workplaces for his community service. He has also participated in many industry–institute linkage programs, connecting his past employers with his alma maters. During the COVID-19 pandemic (which was unfolding at the time of writing of this book), he participated in and led many initiatives to distribute essential supplies and medicine to needy people in his local community.

About the Technical Reviewer

Joos Korstanje is a data scientist with more five years of industry experience in developing machine learning tools, especially forecasting models. He currently works at Disneyland Paris where he develops machine learning for a variety of tools. He is the author of the book *Advanced Forecasting with Python*.

Acknowledgments

I would like to thank Celestin and Aditee for giving me an opportunity to share my knowledge and experience with readers. I thank James Markham for helping me to shape this book according to Apress standards. I am in debt to the technical reviewer for helping me to improve this book. I also thank Prof. Govindrajulu Sir's family, Srinivas (son) and Amy (daughter in law), for allowing me to dedicate this book to his memory and for sharing his biographical information and photograph for publication. I would also like to thank all the people at Apress who were instrumental in bringing this project to reality.

Introduction

I have been working in the domain of data science for more than a decade now, and I was introduced to Python more than 15 years ago. When I first worked with libraries such as NumPy, Matplotlib, and Pandas, I found it a bit tedious to comb through all the available literature in the form of printed books, video tutorials, and online articles, as most of them lacked comprehensive steps for beginners. It was then that I resolved to write a book, and I am glad that I could bring my resolution to life with the help of Apress.

This book is the result of thousands of hours (in addition to the ones spent writing the actual book) going through technical documentation, watching training videos, writing code with the help of different tools, debugging faulty code snippets, posting questions and participating in discussions on various technical forums, and referring to various code repositories for pointers. I have written the book in such a way that beginners will find it easy to understand the topics. The book has hundreds of code examples and images of code output so that you can fully understand each concept introduced. All the code examples are explained in detail.

The book begins with a general discussion of Python and a small guide explaining how to install it on various computing platforms such as the Windows OS and Linux computers (like the Raspberry Pi). We then move on to discussing the scientific ecosystem. Then we focus on NumPy, which is the fundamental library for numerical computing. We specifically focus on the multidimensional, array-like data structure of NumPy, called the *Ndarray*. We then explore data visualization libraries, such as Matplotlib and Plotly, to learn how to plot Ndarrays.

Most of the chapters explore the data visualization library Matplotlib. You will learn a lot of data visualization tips and techniques in these chapters.

Then we dive into Pandas so you can learn about its important data structures, called the *series* and *dataframe*. Midway through the book, you will also learn how to read data from various data sources using Python, NumPy, Matplotlib, and Pandas. You will also learn how to visualize Pandas data with popular visualization libraries such as Matplotlib and Seaborn, as well as how to work with time-indexed data.

On an ending note, we started and finished working on this project at a very turbulent time (the beginning of 2021) marked by hardships such as hospitalization and deaths of friends, social unrest, lockdowns, curfews, economic slowdown, and a host of other sociopolitical problems brought about in part by the COVID-19 pandemic. I myself was hospitalized due to severe complications from pneumonia and breathing troubles caused by a COVID-19 infection. It delayed the launch of this long-planned project. To be frank, working on this book with the help of my longtime mentors at Apress (Celestin, James, and Aditee) offered me a sense of purpose in these troubled times. I end this introduction with a note of hope and positive words that we, as a society and a global civilization, will overcome these turbulent times with the help of each other, and I look at the future with a lot of hope and bright eyes.

CHAPTER 1

Introduction to Python 3

I welcome you all to the exciting journey of data visualization with Matplotlib and related libraries such as NumPy, Pandas, and Seaborn.

This chapter covers the basics of the Python programming language including its history, installation, and applications. You will be writing a few simple and introductory Python 3 programs and be learning how to execute them on various OS platforms.

Then, we will start exploring the scientific Python ecosystem. We will briefly discuss the member libraries of the scientific Python ecosystem, and toward the end, we will explore Jupyter Notebook so we can use it throughout the rest of the book.

Specifically, the following are the topics covered in this chapter:

- Python programming language

- Python installation on various platforms

- Python modes

- Python IDEs

- Scientific Python ecosystem

- Overview and setup of Jupyter Notebook

- Running code in Jupyter Notebook

- Anaconda

After reading this chapter, you will be comfortable with the installation and the basic usage of the Python 3 programming language in various modes on various platforms.

© Ashwin Pajankar 2022
A. Pajankar, *Hands-on Matplotlib*, https://doi.org/10.1007/978-1-4842-7410-1_1

Introducing the Python 3 Programming Language

Python 3 is a general-purpose, high-level, and interpreted programming language. In this section, we will discuss the Python programming language and its philosophy.

History of the Python Programming Language

Python is a successor to the ABC programming language, which itself was inspired by the ALGOL 68 and SETL programming languages. Python was created by Guido van Rossum as a side project during vacations in the late 1980s while he was working at Centrum Wiskunde & Informatica (English: "National Research Institute for Mathematics and Computer Science") in the Netherlands. Van Rossum was born and raised in the Netherlands. He obtained a master's degree in math and computer science from the University of Amsterdam. He worked for Google and Dropbox and retired after that. However, in November 2020, he joined Microsoft.

Since the initial release of the Python programming language till July 2018, Guido has been the lead developer and benevolent dictator for life (BDFL) for this project. He worked on the steering committee for Python through 2019, but in 2020, he withdrew his nomination from reelection to the steering committee.

The following are the important milestones in Python's release timeline:

- *February 1991*: Van Rossum published the code (labeled version 0.9.0) to `alt.sources`.

- *January 1994*: Version 1.0 was released.

- *October 2000*: Python 2.0 was released.

- *December 2006*: Python 3.0 was released.

- *December 2019*: Python 2.*x* was officially retired and is no longer supported by Python Software Foundation.

As you can see, Python 2.*x* versions are no longer supported, as Python 2 is retired. Python 3 is not backward compatible with Python 2. Python 3 is the latest and supported version of the Python programming language. So, we will use Python 3 programming throughout the book to demonstrate the concepts covered. Unless explicitly mentioned, Python means Python 3 throughout this book.

Python Enhancement Proposals

To steer the development, maintenance, and support of Python, the Python leadership came up with the concept of *Python enhancement proposals* (PEPs). They are the primary mechanism for suggesting new features and fixing issues in the Python project. You can read more about the PEPs at the following URLs:

```
https://www.python.org/dev/peps/
https://www.python.org/dev/peps/pep-0001/
```

Philosophy of the Python Programming Language

The philosophy of Python is detailed in PEP20. It is known as the Zen of Python and is at `https://www.python.org/dev/peps/pep-0020/`. The following are the points from that PEP. A few are funny.

- Beautiful is better than ugly.

- Explicit is better than implicit.

- Simple is better than complex.

- Complex is better than complicated.

- Flat is better than nested.

- Sparse is better than dense.

- Readability counts.

- Special cases aren't special enough to break the rules.

  - Although practicality beats purity.

- Errors should never pass silently.

  - Unless explicitly silenced.

- In the face of ambiguity, refuse the temptation to guess.

- There should be one—and preferably only one—obvious way to do it.

  - Although that way may not be obvious at first unless you're Dutch.

- Now is better than never.

    - Although never is often better than *right* now.

- If the implementation is hard to explain, it's a bad idea.

- If the implementation is easy to explain, it may be a good idea.

- Namespaces are one honking great idea—let's do more of those!

These are the general philosophical guidelines that continue to influence the development of the Python programming language.

Applications of Python

As you have learned, Python is a general-purpose programming language; it has numerous applications in the following areas:

- Web development

- GUI development

- Scientific and numerical computing

- Software development

- System administration

You can read case studies of Python at `https://www.python.org/success-stories/`.

Installing Python on Various Platforms

A Python *implementation* is a program (the actual binary executable of the interpreter of Python) that supports the execution of programs written in the Python programming language. The original implementation created by Guido van Russom is known as *CPython* and serves as the reference implementation. Throughout the book, we will be using CPython. It is available on the Python website, and you will learn how to install it on the Windows OS in this section. I prefer to write Python programs on a Windows computer or a Raspberry Pi computer with the Raspberry Pi OS. You can find the list of alternative Python implementations at `https://www.python.org/download/alternatives/`.

I think now is a good time to discuss various Python distributions. You saw that the actual interpreter program for Python is known as an *implementation*. When it is bundled with a few useful things such as an integrated development environment (IDE), tools, and libraries, it is known as a *distribution*. You can find the list of Python distributions at `https://wiki.python.org/moin/PythonDistributions`.

Now, let's look at how to install Python on both platforms.

Installing on a Windows Computer

Visit the Python 3 download page located at `https://www.python.org/downloads/` and download the setup file of Python 3 for your computer. The page will automatically detect the operating system on your computer and show the appropriate downloadable file, as shown in Figure 1-1.

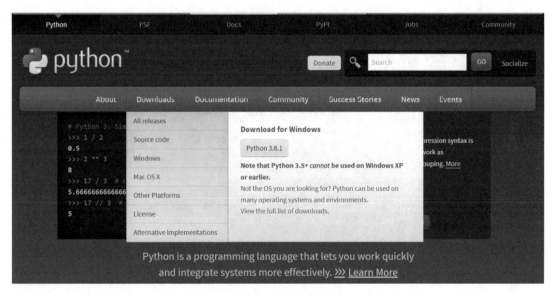

Figure 1-1. *Python project home page with download options*

Run the setup file to install Python 3. During installation, select the check box related to adding Python 3 to the PATH variable (Figure 1-2).

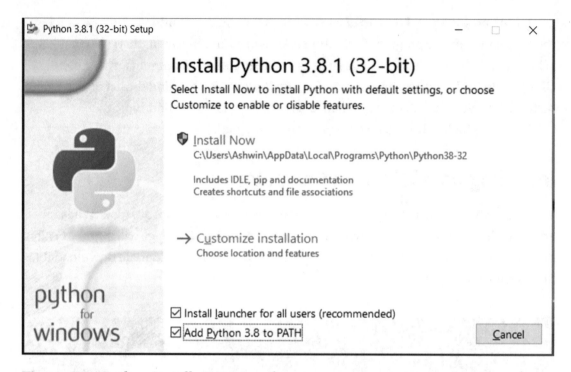

Figure 1-2. *Python installation wizard*

Also, choose the "Customize installation" option. That will take you to more options, as shown in Figure 1-3.

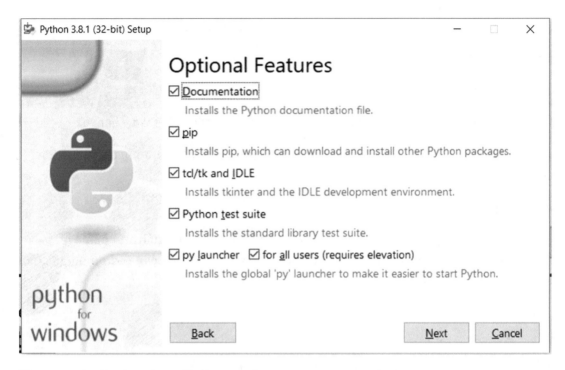

Figure 1-3. *Python installation options*

Select all the boxes and click the Next button to continue the setup. Complete the setup. The name of the binary executable program for Python is python on Windows. Once the installation completes, run the following command at the Windows command prompt, cmd:

```
python -V
```

This will return the version of Python 3 as follows:

```
Python 3.8.1
```

You can also check the version of pip as follows:

```
pip3 -V
```

A recursive acronym, *pip* stands for "Pip installs Python" or "Pip installs packages." It is a package manager for the Python programming language. You can install the other needed Python libraries for our demonstrations using the pip utility.

To find out the exact location of Python, you can run the `where` command as follows:

```
where python
```

This returns the following result:

```
C:\Users\Ashwin\AppData\Local\Programs\Python\Python38-32\python.exe
```

Similarly, you can find out the location of the pip3 utility by running the following command:

```
where pip3
```

We will be using this utility heavily throughout the book to install and manage Python 3 libraries on the computer we are working with. The following command lists all the installed packages:

```
pip3 list
```

Installing on Ubuntu/Debian Derivatives

Debian is a popular distribution. Ubuntu Linux and the Raspberry Pi OS are the other popular distributions based on Debian. Python 3 and pip3 come pre-installed on all the Debian distributions and derivatives such as Ubuntu or the Raspberry Pi OS. So, we do not have to install them separately. I use the Raspberry Pi OS on a Raspberry Pi 4B with 8 GB RAM as my Linux computer. Both the major Python versions, Python 2 and Python 3, come preinstalled on all the Debian derivatives. Their executable files for interpreters are named as `python` and `python3` for Python 2 and Python 3, respectively. We will use `python3` for our demonstrations. To find out the versions and locations of the needed binary executable files, run the following commands one by one:

```
python3 -V
pip3 -V
which python3
which pip3
```

Almost all the other popular Linux distributions come with Python pre-installed too.

Using Python Modes

The Python programming language has various modes for executing programs (and statements, as you will see soon). Let's discuss them one by one. But before we get started with that discussion, let's look at what IDLE is. IDLE is an integrated development and learning environment developed by the Python Software Foundation for Python programming. When you install the CPython implementation of Python 3 on Windows, IDLE is also installed. You can launch it on Windows OS in various ways. The first way is to search for it in the Windows search bar by typing in **IDLE**, as shown in Figure 1-4.

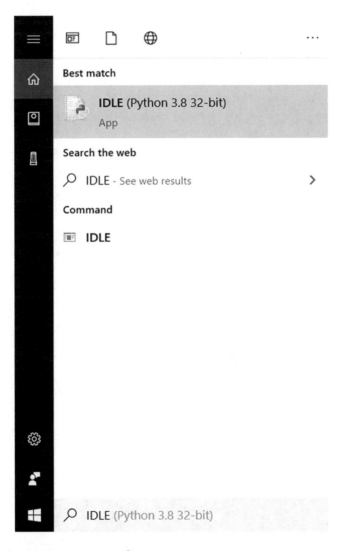

Figure 1-4. *Python IDLE on Windows*

The other way is to launch it from the command prompt (cmd) by running the following command:

```
idle
```

This will launch the window shown in Figure 1-5.

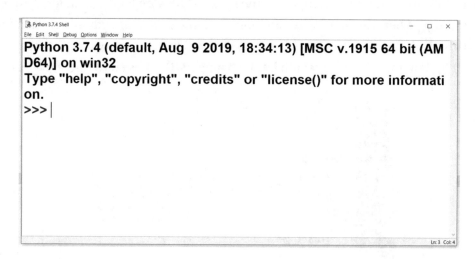

Figure 1-5. *Python IDLE*

Before proceeding, you need to customize IDLE so that it works for you. You can change the font by selecting Options ➤ Configure IDLE, as shown in Figure 1-6.

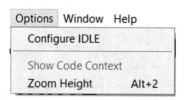

Figure 1-6. *Configuring IDLE*

The window shown in Figure 1-7 opens so you can change the font and size of the characters in IDLE.

Figure 1-7. *IDLE configuration window*

Adjust the options according to your own preferences.

All the Linux distributions may not come with IDLE pre-installed. You can install it on the Debian and derivatives (Ubuntu and Raspberry Pi OS) by running the following commands in sequence:

```
sudo apt-get update
sudo apt-get install idle3
```

Once the installation is complete, you can find IDLE in the menu (in this case the Raspberry Pi OS menu), as shown in Figure 1-8.

Figure 1-8. *IDLE in Raspberry Pi OS menu*

You can also launch IDLE on Linux by running the following command:

```
idle
```

Now let's discuss the various modes of Python.

Interactive Mode

Python's interactive mode is like a command-line shell that executes the current statement and gives immediate feedback on the console. It runs the statements given to it immediately. As new statements are fed into and executed by the interpreter, the code is evaluated. When you open IDLE, you will see a command-line prompt. This is Python's interactive mode. To see a simple example, let's type in the customary **Hello World** program in the interactive prompt as follows:

```
print('Hello World!')
```

Press the Enter key to feed the line to the interpreter and execute it. Figure 1-9 shows the output.

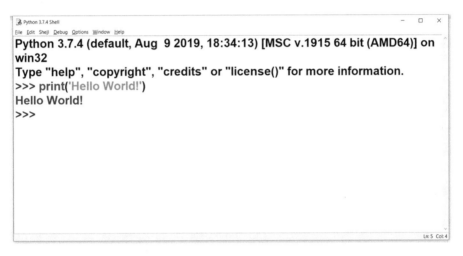

Figure 1-9. *Python interactive mode on IDLE*

You can launch Python's interactive mode from the command prompt too. At the Linux command prompt (e.g., lxterminal), run the command python3, and at the Windows command prompt (cmd), run the command python. Figure 1-10 shows the interactive mode at the Windows command prompt.

```
C:\Users\Ashwin>python
Python 3.8.3 (tags/v3.8.3:6f8c832, May 13 2020, 22:20:19) [MSC
v.1925 32 bit (Intel)] on win32
Type "help", "copyright", "credits" or "license" for more infor
mation.
>>> ▄
```

Figure 1-10. *Python interactive mode, Windows command prompt*

Script Mode

You can write a Python program and save it to disk. Then you can launch it in multiple ways. This is known as *script mode*. Let's demonstrate it in IDLE. You can use any text editor to write the Python program. But as IDLE is an IDE, it is convenient to write and run the Python programs using IDLE. Let's see that first. In IDLE, select File ➤ New File. This will create a new blank file. Add the following code to it:

```python
print('Hello World!')
```

Then save it with the name prog01.py on the disk (Figure 1-11).

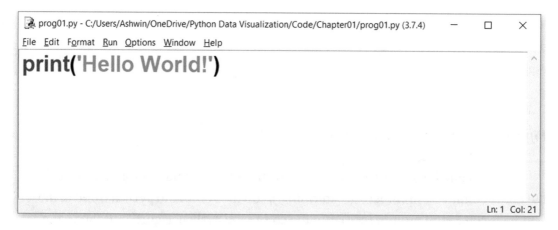

Figure 1-11. *A Python program in the IDLE code editor*

In the menu, select Run ➤ Run Module. This will execute the program at IDLE's prompt, as shown in Figure 1-12.

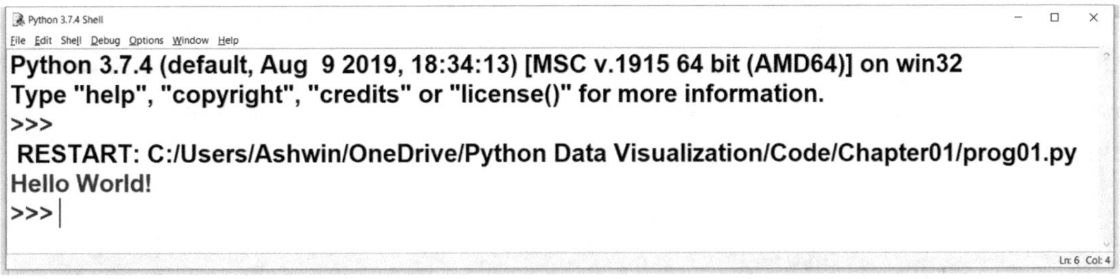

Figure 1-12. *A Python program under execution at the IDLE prompt*

You can even launch the program with Python's interpreter at the command prompt of the OS. Open the command prompt of the OS and navigate to the directory where the program is stored. At the Windows command prompt, run the following command:

```
python prog01.py
```

In the Linux terminal, you must run the following command prompt:

```
python3 prog01.py
```

Then the interpreter will run the program at the command prompt, and the output (if any) will appear there.

In Linux, there is another way you can run the program without explicitly using the interpreter. You can add a shebang line to the beginning of the code file. For example, say our code file looks like this:

```
#!/usr/bin/python3
print('Hello World!')
```

The first line is known as a *shebang* line. It tells the shell what interpreter to use and its location. Then run the following command to change the file permission to make it executable for the owner as follows:

```
chmod 755 prog01.py
```

Then you can directly launch your Python program file like any other executable with ./, as follows:

```
./prog01.py
```

The shell will execute the program and print the output in the terminal. Note that this is applicable only for Unix-like systems (Linux and macOS) as they support executing programs like this. You will learn more about Python programming throughout the book.

Using Python IDEs

You have learned how to work with the Python interpreter and IDLE to run Python 3 statements and programs. You can use other freely available IDEs and plugins for IDEs to work with Python. The following is a list of a few famous IDEs and plugins for Python 3 along with the URLs to their home pages:

- PyCharm Community Edition (`https://www.jetbrains.com/pycharm/`)

- Spyder IDE (`https://www.spyder-ide.org/`)

- Thonny Python Editor (`https://thonny.org/`)

- Mu Editor (`https://codewith.mu/`)

- PyDev plugin for Eclipse (`https://www.pydev.org/`)

All these IDEs and plugins are free to download and use. As an exercise for this chapter, you may want to explore them to find the IDE you are most comfortable with.

Exploring the Scientific Python Ecosystem

The scientific Python ecosystem is a collection of open source Python libraries for scientific computing. It has the following core components:

- *Python*: This is a programming language.

- *NumPy*: This is the fundamental library for numerical computation. Almost all the libraries in the scientific Python ecosystem are based on NumPy. It provides a versatile data structure known as an *Ndarray* (for "N-dimensional array").

- *SciPy*: This library has many routines for scientific computations.

- *Matplotlib*: This is a library for visualization. Its `pyplot` module has routines for Matlab-style visualizations.

Together, all these components provide functionality like Matlab:

Pandas: This is a library for data science and provides high-performance, easy-to-use data structures like the series and dataframes for storing data.

SymPy: This is for symbolic mathematics and algebra.

NetworkX: This is a library for representing and visualizing graphs and networks.

Scikit-image: This is a library for image processing.

Scikit-learn: This is a library for machine learning and artificial intelligence.

In addition to these libraries, IPython provides a better interactive environment for the Python interpreter. IPython's interactive environment can be accessed through web-based notebooks using Jupyter Notebook.

The rest of the chapter focuses on Jupyter Notebook.

Introducing Jupyter Notebook

Earlier in this chapter, you learned various ways to run Python statements. You ran Python statements in a script and in the interpreter's interactive mode. The main advantage of using interactive mode is the immediate feedback. The main disadvantage of this mode is that if you make any mistakes in the statements you're typing in, you must write the entire statement again to re-execute it. Also, it is difficult to save it as a program. The option for saving the statements to run on the interpreter can be found in the File option of the menu. However, all the statements and their outputs will be saved in plain-text format with the `.py` extension. If there is any graphical output, it is displayed separately and cannot be stored with the statements.

Because of the limitations of interactive mode in the interpreter, we will use a better tool for running the Python statements interactively in the web browser. The tool is known as Jupyter Notebook. It is a server program that can create interactive notebooks in a web browser.

Jupyter Notebook is a web-based notebook that is used for interactive programming of various programming languages like Python, Octave, Julia, and R. It is popular with people who are working in research domains. Jupyter Notebook can save code, visualizations, output, and rich text in a single file. The advantage of Jupyter Notebook over Python's own interactive prompt is that you can edit the code and see the new output instantly, which is not possible in Python's interactive mode. Another advantage is that you have the code, rich-text elements, and output of the code (which can be in graphical or rich-text format) in the same file on disk. This makes it easy to distribute. You can save and share these notebooks over the Internet or using the portable storage equipment. There are many services online that help to store and execute your notebook scripts on cloud servers.

Setting Up Jupyter Notebook

You can easily install the Jupyter Notebook server program on any computer by running the following command at the command prompt:

```
pip3 install jupyter
```

Let's see how you can use Jupyter Notebook for writing and executing Python statements now. Run the following command in the command prompt of the OS to launch the Jupyter Notebook server process there:

```
jupyter notebook
```

The Jupyter Notebook server process will be launched, and the command prompt window shows a server log, as in Figure 1-13.

```
pi@raspberrypi:~ $ jupyter notebook
[I 10:02:23.804 NotebookApp] Serving notebooks from local directory: /home/pi
[I 10:02:23.804 NotebookApp] The Jupyter Notebook is running at:
[I 10:02:23.804 NotebookApp] http://localhost:8888/?token=72f78afdadcf74d58dc766
6b45e8dede2b7721c53abeee4d
[I 10:02:23.804 NotebookApp]  or http://127.0.0.1:8888/?token=72f78afdadcf74d58d
c7666b45e8dede2b7721c53abeee4d
[I 10:02:23.804 NotebookApp] Use Control-C to stop this server and shut down all
 kernels (twice to skip confirmation).
[C 10:02:23.877 NotebookApp]

    To access the notebook, open this file in a browser:
        file:///home/pi/.local/share/jupyter/runtime/nbserver-9026-open.html
    Or copy and paste one of these URLs:
        http://localhost:8888/?token=72f78afdadcf74d58dc7666b45e8dede2b7721c53ab
eee4d
      or http://127.0.0.1:8888/?token=72f78afdadcf74d58dc7666b45e8dede2b7721c53ab
eee4d
```

Figure 1-13. *Launching a new Jupyter Notebook process*

Also, it launches a web page in the default browser of the OS. If the browser window is already open, then it launches the page in a new tab of the same browser window. Another way to open the page (in case you close this browser window running Jupyter Notebook) is to visit http://localhost:8888/ in your browser. It displays the page shown in Figure 1-14.

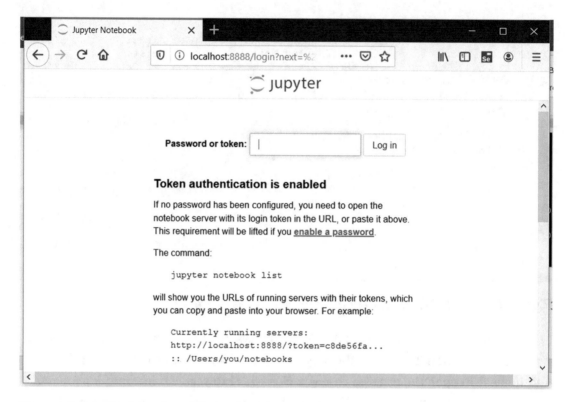

Figure 1-14. *Logging in with a token*

The following lines of text are the server logs.

To access the notebook, open this file in a browser:

file:///C:/Users/Ashwin/AppData/Roaming/jupyter/runtime/nbserver-8420-open.html

Or copy and paste one of these URLs:

http://localhost:8888/?token=e4a4fab0d8c22cd01b6530d5daced19d32d7e0c3a56f925c
http://127.0.0.1:8888/?token=e4a4fab0d8c22cd01b6530d5daced19d32d7e0c3a56f925c

In the previous log, you can see a couple of URLs. They refer to the same page (localhost and 127.0.0.1 are the same hosts). Either you can directly copy and paste any of these URLs directly in the address bar of the browser tab and open the Jupyter Notebook home page or you can visit http://localhost:8888/ as discussed earlier and then paste the token in the server log (in our case it is e4a4fab0d8c22cd01b6530d5daced19d32d7e0c3a56f925c) and log in. This will take you to the same home page.

Note that every instance of the Jupyter Notebook server will have its own token, so the token shown in the book will not work with your notebook. The token is valid only for that server process.

So, if you follow any one of the routes explained earlier, you will see a home page tab in the browser window, as shown in Figure 1-15.

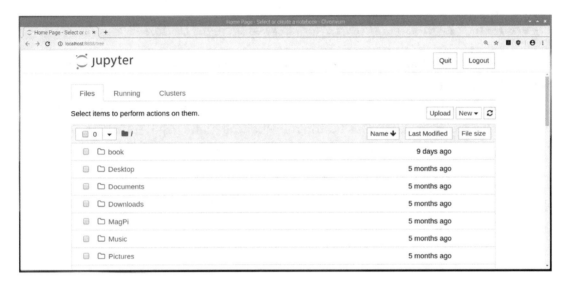

Figure 1-15. *A new home page tab of Jupyter Notebook*

As you can see, there are three tabs on the web page: Files, Running, and Clusters. The Files tab shows the directories and files in the directory from where you launched the notebook server from the command prompt. In the previous example, I executed the command `jupyter notebook` from lxterminal of my Raspberry Pi. And the current working directory is the home directory of the `pi` user `/home/pi`. That is why you can see all the files and directories in the home directory of my Raspberry Pi computer in Figure 1-15.

In the top-right corner, you can see the Quit and Logout buttons. If you click the Logout button, then it logs out from the current session, and to log in, you again need the token or URL with the embedded token from the notebook server log, as discussed earlier. If you click the Quit button, then it stops the notebook server process running at the command prompt and displays the modal message box shown in Figure 1-16.

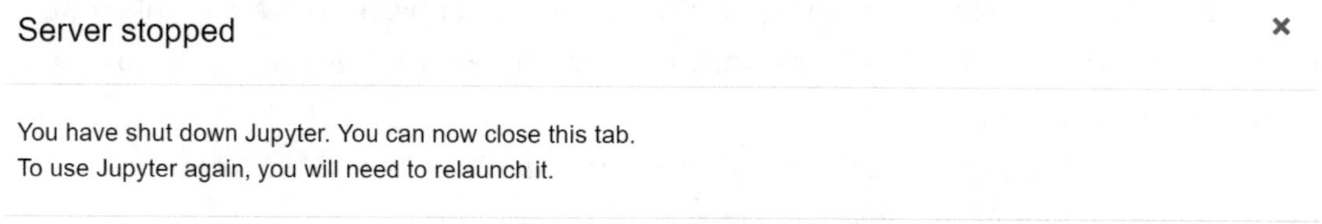

Server stopped   ✕

You have shut down Jupyter. You can now close this tab.
To use Jupyter again, you will need to relaunch it.

Figure 1-16. *The message shown after clicking the Quit button*

To work with the Jupyter Notebook, you need to execute the command `jupyter notebook` again at the command prompt.

On the top-right side, just below the Quit and Logout buttons, you can see a small button with a refresh symbol. This button refreshes the home page. You also have the New button. Once clicked, it shows a drop-down, as shown in Figure 1-17.

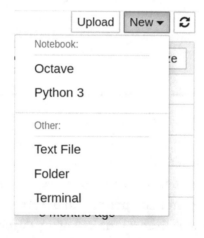

Figure 1-17. *Options for a new notebook*

As you can see, the drop-down is divided into two sections, Notebook and Other. You can create the Octave and Python 3 notebooks. If your computer has more programming languages installed that are supported by Jupyter Notebook, then all those languages will show up here. You can also create text files and folders. You can open a command prompt in the web browser by clicking Terminal. Figure 1-18 shows lxterminal running in a separate web browser tab.

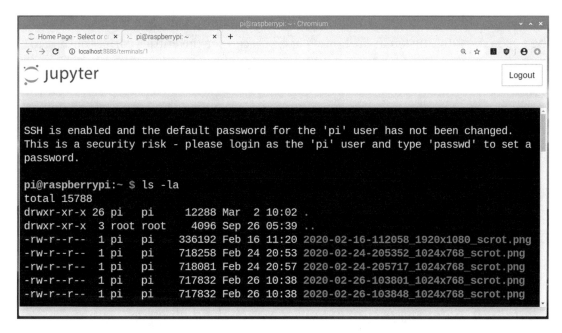

Figure 1-18. *A new lxterminal window within the browser*

Clicking Python 3 in the drop-down creates a new Python 3 notebook, as shown in Figure 1-19.

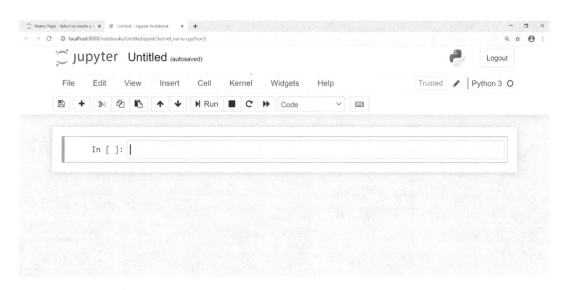

Figure 1-19. *A new Python 3 notebook*

If you go to the home page again by clicking the home page tab in the browser and then open the Running tab in the home page, you can see the entries corresponding to the terminal and the Python 3 notebook, as shown in Figure 1-20.

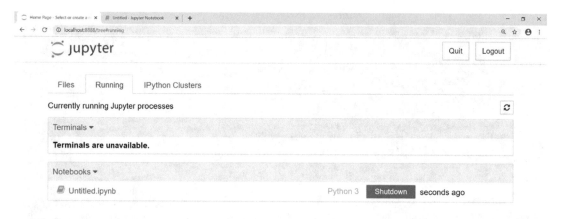

Figure 1-20. *Summary of current Jupyter Notebook subprocesses*

Running Code in Jupyter Notebook

Go to Python 3's Untitled1 tab again and type in the following statement in the text area (also known as a *cell*):

```
printf("Hello, World!\n");
```

Then click the Run button. Jupyter will execute the statement as a Python 3 statement and show the result immediately below the cell, as shown in Figure 1-21.

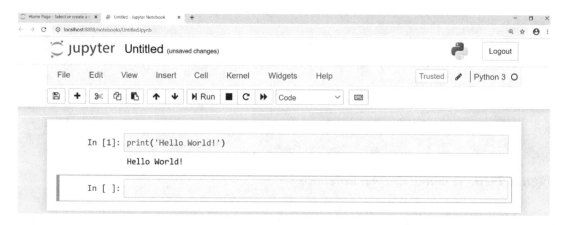

Figure 1-21. *Code output in Jupyter Notebook*

As you can see, after execution, it automatically creates a new cell below the result and sets the cursor there. Let's discuss the menu bar and the icons above the programming cells. You can save the file by clicking the floppy disk icon. You can add a new empty cell after the current cell by clicking the + icon. The next three icons are Cut, Copy, and Paste. Using the up and down arrows can shift the position of the current cell up and down, respectively. The next option is to run the cell, which you already saw. The next three icons are for interrupting the kernel, restarting the kernel, and rerunning all the cells in the notebook. Next to that, you have a drop-down that tells you what type of cell it should be. Figure 1-22 shows the drop-down when clicked.

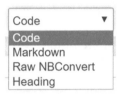

Figure 1-22. *Types of cells in Jupyter Notebook*

The cell is treated as a Python 3 code cell when you choose the Code option. It is treated as a Markdown cell when you choose the Markdown option. Markdown is a markup language that can create rich-text output. For example, anything followed by # creates a heading, anything followed by ## creates a subheading, and so on. Just type the following lines in a Markdown cell and execute them:

```
# Heading 1
## Heading 2
```

During our Python 3 demonstrations, we will mostly use Markdown for headings. However, you can further explore Markdown on your own by visiting `https://jupyter-notebook.readthedocs.io/en/stable/examples/Notebook/Working%20With%20Markdown%20Cells.html`. Figure 1-23 shows the output of the previous demonstration.

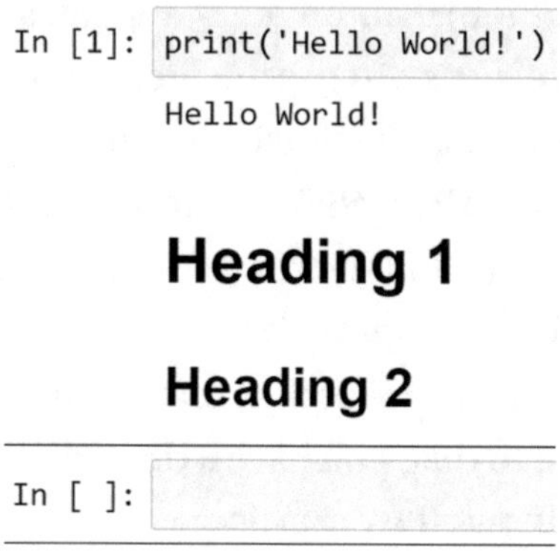

```
In [1]:  print('Hello World!')
         Hello World!
```

Heading 1

Heading 2

```
In [ ]:
```

Figure 1-23. *Headings in Markdown*

You can even change the name of the notebook file by clicking its name in the top part of the notebook. Once you click, you'll see a modal box for renaming, as shown in Figure 1-24.

Rename Notebook   ✕

Enter a new notebook name:

Untitled1

                                                          Cancel   Rename

Figure 1-24. *Renaming a notebook in Jupyter*

Rename the notebook if you want. If you browse the location on disk from where you launched the Jupyter Notebook from at the command prompt, you will find the file with the `.ipynb` extension (meaning "IPython notebook").

In the same way, you can use Jupyter Notebook for doing interactive programming with the other programming languages that support Jupyter. We will mostly use this notebook format to store our code snippets for interactive sessions. This is because everything is saved in a single file that can be shared easily, as discussed earlier.

You can clear the output of a cell or the entire notebook. In the menu bar, click the Cell menu. In the drop-down, Current Outputs and All Output have a Clear option that clears the output of cells. Figure 1-25 shows the options.

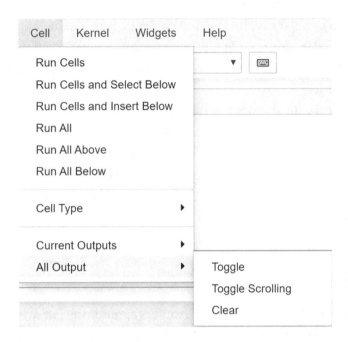

Figure 1-25. *Clearing the output in Jupyter*

One of the most significant advantages of Jupyter Notebook is that you can edit an already executed cell if there is any syntax error or you simply want to change the code. Jupyter Notebook is like an IDE that runs within a web browser and produces the output in the same window. This interactivity and facility to keep code, rich text, and output in the same file has made Jupyter Notebook project hugely popular worldwide. The kernel for running Python programs comes from the IPython project. As I mentioned earlier, you can use it for other programming languages too. I have used it for running GNU Octave programs.

You can find more information about Jupyter Notebook and IPython at the following URLs:

```
https://jupyter.org/
https://ipython.org/
```

Anaconda

Before we can conclude the chapter, we need to discuss the Python distributions. A Python distribution is nothing more than the Python interpreter bundled with Python libraries. One such popular distribution is Anaconda. You can download and install Anaconda on Linux, Windows, and macOS. Anaconda has many versions. One of them is free and meant for individual usage. You can find it at `https://www.anaconda.com/products/individual`.

Anaconda comes with an open source package manager that can install packages for Python and other programs. It is known as Conda. You can find more information about the Conda package manager at `https://docs.conda.io/en/latest/`.

If you have already installed Python from Python's website, I recommend using another computer to install Anaconda. Having multiple interpreters and distributions of Python can be confusing.

Summary

In this chapter, you learned the basics of Python programming language. You learned how to write basic Python programs and how to execute them in various ways. You learned to work with Python on various operating systems such as Windows and Linux. You also learned various modes of the Python programming language and how to launch Python from the command prompts of various operating systems. You learned the basics of the built-in package manager of Python, called pip. We also briefly discussed other IDEs for Python.

Then, you got a brief introduction to the scientific Python ecosystem. We will explore many components of this ecosystem in the coming chapters. You also learned how to install Jupyter Notebook on various platforms and explored how you can run simple Python statements in Jupyter Notebook. You learned that you can store the code and the output of the same code in a single file that can be shared easily over the Internet and other media such as portable storage devices.

In the next chapter, we will get started with NumPy.

CHAPTER 2

Getting Started with NumPy

In the previous chapter, you learned the basics of the Python programming language and the scientific Python ecosystem. You also learned how to run simple Python programs in interactive web-based notebooks with Jupyter. We will continue using Jupyter Notebook for the majority of demonstrations in the rest of the chapters in the book.

In this chapter, we will give a brief overview of the NumPy library with a few coding demonstrations. The following is the list of topics that we will explore in this chapter:

- Introduction to the NumPy Ndarrays

- Ndarray properties

- NumPy constants

Throughout the remaining chapters of this book, we will explore many components of the scientific Python ecosystem one by one. Throughout this book, we will be using different libraries that are part of this scientific Python ecosystem. The valuable knowledge you will gain in this chapter serves as a foundation for the rest of the chapters. As this is an introductory chapter for a broad ecosystem, I have kept it short yet practical.

NumPy and Ndarrays

NumPy is the fundamental package for numerical computation in Python. We can use it for numerical computations. The most useful feature of the NumPy library is the multidimensional container data structure known as an *Ndarray*.

An Ndarray is a multidimensional array (also known as a *container*) of items that have the same datatype and size. We can define the size and datatype of the items at the time of creating the Ndarray. Just like other data structures such as lists, we can access the contents of an Ndarray with an index. The index in an Ndarray starts at 0 (just like arrays in C or lists in Python). We can use Ndarrays for a variety of computations. All the

29

© Ashwin Pajankar 2022
A. Pajankar, *Hands-on Matplotlib*, https://doi.org/10.1007/978-1-4842-7410-1_2

other libraries in the scientific Python ecosystem recognize and utilize NumPy Ndarrays and associated routines to represent their own data structures and operations on them.

Let's get started with the hands-on material. Create a new notebook for this chapter. Run the following command to install the NumPy library on your computer:

```
!pip3 install numpy
```

Let's import it to the current notebook by running the following command:

```
import numpy as np
```

You can create a list and use it to create a simple Ndarray as follows:

```
l1 = [1, 2, 3]
x = np.array(l1, dtype=np.int16)
```

Here you are creating an Ndarray from a list. The datatype of the members is a 16-bit integer. You can find the detailed list of datatypes supported at https://numpy.org/devdocs/user/basics.types.html.

You can write the previous code in a single line as follows:

```
x = np.array([1, 2, 3], dtype=np.int16)
```

Let's print the value of the Ndarray and its type (which, we know, is an Ndarray).

```
print(x)
print(type(x))
```

The output is as follows:

```
[1 2 3]
<class 'numpy.ndarray'>
```

As you can observe in the previous output, it is of the class numpy.ndarray.

You can also use Python's interactive mode for running all the statements, as shown in Figure 2-1.

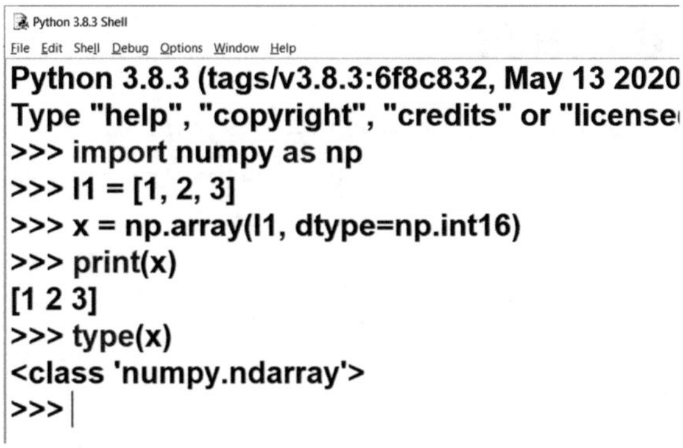

```
Python 3.8.3 Shell
File  Edit  Shell  Debug  Options  Window  Help
Python 3.8.3 (tags/v3.8.3:6f8c832, May 13 2020
Type "help", "copyright", "credits" or "license
>>> import numpy as np
>>> l1 = [1, 2, 3]
>>> x = np.array(l1, dtype=np.int16)
>>> print(x)
[1 2 3]
>>> type(x)
<class 'numpy.ndarray'>
>>>
```

Figure 2-1. *Running the example code in interactive mode in the Python shell*

You can run most of the code examples you will practice in this book in the Python shell too. Similarly, you can launch the IPython shell by typing the command `ipython` at the command prompt and then run the code examples, as shown in Figure 2-2.

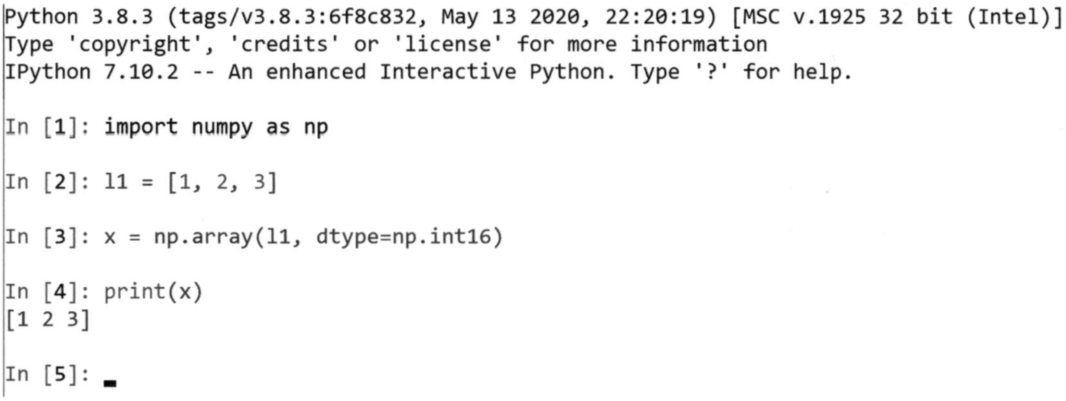

```
Python 3.8.3 (tags/v3.8.3:6f8c832, May 13 2020, 22:20:19) [MSC v.1925 32 bit (Intel)]
Type 'copyright', 'credits' or 'license' for more information
IPython 7.10.2 -- An enhanced Interactive Python. Type '?' for help.

In [1]: import numpy as np

In [2]: l1 = [1, 2, 3]

In [3]: x = np.array(l1, dtype=np.int16)

In [4]: print(x)
[1 2 3]

In [5]:
```

Figure 2-2. *Running the example code in interactive mode in the IPython shell*

While you can use the Python interactive shell and IPython for running the code examples, it is not possible to save the code, output, and other assets (like rich-text titles) in a single file with these tools, so we will mostly be using Jupyter Notebook files (`*.ipynb` files) in this book. We will also be using Python script mode programs (`*.py` files) in a few cases.

Indexing in Ndarrays

Let's take a brief look at the indexing of Ndarrays. As you learned earlier briefly, the indexing starts at 0. Let's demonstrate that by accessing the members of the Ndarray as follows:

```
print(x[0]); print(x[1]); print(x[2])
```

The output is as follows:

```
1
2
3
```

You can even use a negative index: -1 returns the last element, -2 returns the second last, and so on. The following is an example:

```
print(x[-1])
```

If you provide any invalid index, then it throws an error.

```
print(x[3])
```

In the previous statement, you are trying to access the fourth element in the Ndarray, which is nonexistent. This returns the following error:

```
IndexError                    Traceback (most recent call last)
<ipython-input-4-d3c02b9c2b5d> in <module>
----> 1 print(x[3])

IndexError: index 3 is out of bounds for axis 0 with size 3
```

Indexing in Ndarrays of More Than One Dimension

You can have more than one dimensions for an array as follows:

```
x1 = np.array([[1, 2, 3], [4, 5, 6]], np.int16)
```

The previous is a two-dimensional matrix. It has two rows and three columns. You can access individual elements as follows:

```
print(x1[0, 0]); print(x1[0, 1]); print(x1[0, 2]);
```

You can even access entire rows as follows:

```
print(x1[0, :])
print(x1[1, :])
```

The output is as follows:

```
[1 2 3]
[4 5 6]
```

You can access an entire column as follows:

```
print(x[:, 0])
```

The output is as follows:

```
[1 4]
```

You can even have an Ndarray with more than two dimensions. The following is a 3D array:

```
x2 = np.array([[[1, 2, 3], [4, 5, 6]],[[0, -1, -2], [-3, -4, -5]]],
np.int16)
```

In scientific and business applications, you'll often have multidimensional data. Ndarrays are useful for storing numerical data. Try to run the following items and retrieve the elements of the previous 3D matrix:

```
print(x2[0, 0, 0])
print(x2[1, 1, 2])
print(x2[:, 1, 1])
```

Ndarray Properties

You can learn more about the Ndarrays by referring to their properties. Let's see all the properties in action by looking at a demonstration. Specifically, let's use the same 3D matrix we used earlier.

```
x2 = np.array([[[1, 2, 3], [4, 5, 6]],[[0, -1, -2], [-3, -4, -5]]], np.int16)
```

You can find out the number of dimensions with the following statement:

```
print(x2.ndim)
```

The output returns the number of dimensions.

```
3
```

You can find out the shape of the Ndarray as follows:

```
print(x2.shape)
```

The shape means the size of the dimensions as follows:

```
(2, 2, 3)
```

You can find out the datatype of the members as follows:

```
print(x2.dtype)
```

The output is as follows:

```
int16
```

You can find out the size (number of elements) and the number of bytes required in the memory for the storage as follows:

```
print(x2.size)
print(x2.nbytes)
```

The output is as follows:

```
12
24
```

You can compute the transpose with the following code:

```
print(x2.T)
```

NumPy Constants

The NumPy library has many useful mathematical and scientific constants you can use in your programs. The following code snippet prints all such important constants.

The following code snippet refers to infinity:

```
print(np.inf)
```

The following code snippet refers to Not a Number:

```
print(np.NAN)
```

The following code snippet refers to negative infinity:

```
print(np.NINF)
```

The following code snippet refers to negative and positive zeros:

```
print(np.NZERO)
print(np.PZERO)
```

The following code snippet refers to Euler's number:

```
print(np.e)
```

The following code snippet refers to Euler's gamma and pi:

```
print(np.euler_gamma)
print(np.pi)
```

The output is as follows:

```
inf
nan
-inf
-0.0
0.0
2.718281828459045
0.5772156649015329
3.141592653589793
```

Slicing Ndarrays

Let's see examples of slicing operations on Ndarrays. You can extract a part of an Ndarray with slicing using indices as follows:

```
a1 = np.array([1, 2, 3, 4, 5, 6, 7])
a1[1:5]
```

This code will display the elements from the second position to the sixth position (you know that the 0 is the starting index) as follows:

```
array([2, 3, 4, 5])
```

You can show the elements from the fourth position as follows:

```
a1[3:]
```

The output is as follows:

```
array([4, 5, 6, 7])
```

You can also show all the elements up to a particular index (excluding the element at that index) as follows:

```
a1[:3]
```

The output is as follows:

```
array([1, 2, 3])
```

You saw the use of negative indices. We can use them for slicing as follows:

```
a1[-4:-1]
```

The output is as follows:

```
array([4, 5, 6])
```

You have been slicing the data with a step size of 1. This means you are retrieving the continuous elements in the resultset. You can also change the step size as follows:

```
a1[1:6:2]
```

In this example, the size of the step is 2. So, the output will list every second (every other) element. The output is as follows:

```
array([2, 4, 6])
```

Summary

In this chapter, you started learning the basics of NumPy and Ndarrays. This is a big library with lots of routines. There are entire books dedicated to NumPy. However, our publishing constraints won't warrant that sort of exploration of this useful library. We will explore more routines from the NumPy library in the coming chapters as and when we need them for our visualization demonstrations.

In the next chapter, you will learn about a few Ndarray creation routines and the basics of data visualization with Matplotlib.

CHAPTER 3

NumPy Routines and Getting Started with Matplotlib

In the previous chapter, you learned the basics of NumPy. Specifically, you learned how to install it and how to create Ndarrays. All the topics you learned in the previous chapter will serve as a foundation for the remaining chapters, as the Ndarray is the fundamental data structure that we will be using throughout the book.

In this chapter, we will continue where we left off in the previous chapter and look at a few Ndarray creation routines. We will also get started with the main data visualization library in the scientific computing ecosystem, Matplotlib. We will use the Ndarray creation routines of NumPy to demonstrate visualizations with Matplotlib. This is a detailed chapter with a lot of emphasis on programming and visualizations. The following are the topics you will learn about in this chapter:

- Routines for creating Ndarrays

- Matplotlib

- Visualization with NumPy and Matplotlib

Throughout the remaining chapters of this book, we will frequently use Matplotlib and NumPy to demonstrate data visualization.

© Ashwin Pajankar 2022
A. Pajankar, *Hands-on Matplotlib*, https://doi.org/10.1007/978-1-4842-7410-1_3

Routines for Creating Ndarrays

Let's learn to create Ndarrays of 1s and 0s. We will explore many array creation routines in this section. Use Jupyter Notebook to create a new notebook to save the code for this chapter. np.empty() returns a new array of a given shape and type, without initializing entries. As the entries corresponding to the members are not initialized, they are arbitrary (random). Let's see a small demonstration. Type the following code in a cell in the notebook and run it:

```
import numpy as np
x = np.empty([3, 3], np.uint8)
print(x)
```

The output will be as follows:

```
[[ 64 244  49]
 [  4   1   0]
 [  0   0 124]]
```

Note that the values will be different for every instance of execution as it does not initialize the values upon the creation of the matrix. You can create a matrix of any size as follows:

```
x = np.empty([3, 3, 3], np.uint8)
print(x)
```

The function np.eye() returns a 2D matrix with 1s on the diagonal and 0s for other elements. The following is an example:

```
y = np.eye(5, dtype=np.uint8)
print(y)
```

The output is as follows:

```
[[1 0 0 0 0]
 [0 1 0 0 0]
 [0 0 1 0 0]
 [0 0 0 1 0]
 [0 0 0 0 1]]
```

You can change the position of the index of the diagonal. The default is 0, which refers to the main diagonal. A positive value means an upper diagonal. A negative value means a lower diagonal. The following are examples. Let's demonstrate the upper diagonal first:

```
y = np.eye(5, dtype=np.uint8, k=1)
print(y)
```

The output is as follows:

```
[[0 1 0 0 0]
 [0 0 1 0 0]
 [0 0 0 1 0]
 [0 0 0 0 1]
 [0 0 0 0 0]]
```

The following is the code to demonstrate the lower diagonal:

```
y = np.eye(5, dtype=np.uint8, k=-1)
print(y)
```

The output is as follows:

```
[[0 0 0 0 0]
 [1 0 0 0 0]
 [0 1 0 0 0]
 [0 0 1 0 0]
 [0 0 0 1 0]]
```

An *identity matrix* is a matrix where all the elements at the diagonal are 1 and the rest of the elements are 0. The function np.identity() returns an identity matrix of the specified size, as shown here:

```
x = np.identity(5, dtype= np.uint8)
print(x)
```

The previous code produces the same output as the following code:

```
y = np.eye(5, dtype=np.uint8)
print(y)
```

The output of both the methods will be as follows:

```
[[1 0 0 0 0]
 [0 1 0 0 0]
 [0 0 1 0 0]
 [0 0 0 1 0]
 [0 0 0 0 1]]
```

The function np.ones() returns the matrix of the given size that has all the elements as 1s.

```
x = np.ones((2, 5, 5), dtype=np.int16)
print(x)
```

Run the code and you will see the following output:

```
[[[1 1 1 1 1]
  [1 1 1 1 1]
  [1 1 1 1 1]
  [1 1 1 1 1]
  [1 1 1 1 1]]

 [[1 1 1 1 1]
  [1 1 1 1 1]
  [1 1 1 1 1]
  [1 1 1 1 1]
  [1 1 1 1 1]]]
```

The function np.zeroes() returns a matrix of a given size with all the element as 0s.

```
x = np.zeros((2, 5, 5, 2), dtype=np.int16)
print(x)
```

Run the code and check the output.

The function np.full() returns a new array of a given shape and type, filled with the passed argument. Here's an example:

```
x = np.full((3, 3, 3), dtype=np.int16, fill_value = 5)
print(x)
```

The output is as follows:

```
[[[5 5 5]
  [5 5 5]
  [5 5 5]]

 [[5 5 5]
  [5 5 5]
  [5 5 5]]

 [[5 5 5]
  [5 5 5]
  [5 5 5]]]
```

A *lower triangular matrix* is where the diagonal and all the elements below the diagonal are 1 and the rest of the elements are 0. The function np.tri() returns a lower triangular matrix of a given size, as shown here:

```
x = np.tri(3, 3, k=0, dtype=np.uint16)
print(x)
```

The output is as follows:

```
[[1 0 0]
 [1 1 0]
 [1 1 1]]
```

You can even change the position of the subdiagonal. All the elements below the subdiagonal will be 0.

```
x = np.tri(5, 5, k=1, dtype=np.uint16)
print(x)
```

The output is as follows:

```
[[1 1 0 0 0]
 [1 1 1 0 0]
 [1 1 1 1 0]
 [1 1 1 1 1]
 [1 1 1 1 1]]
```

Another example with a negative value for the subdiagonal is as follows:

```
x = np.tri(5, 5, k=-1, dtype=np.uint16)
print(x)
```

The output is as follows:

```
[[0 0 0 0 0]
 [1 0 0 0 0]
 [1 1 0 0 0]
 [1 1 1 0 0]
 [1 1 1 1 0]]
```

Similarly, you can work with the function np.tril() to obtain a lower triangular matrix. It accepts another matrix as an argument. Here's a demonstration:

```
x = np.ones((5, 5), dtype=np.uint8)
y = np.tril(x, k=-1)
print(y)
```

The output is as follows:

```
[[0 0 0 0 0]
 [1 0 0 0 0]
 [1 1 0 0 0]
 [1 1 1 0 0]
 [1 1 1 1 0]]
```

An upper triangular matrix is where the diagonal and all the elements above are 1 and the rest of the elements are 0.

```
x = np.ones((5, 5), dtype=np.uint8)
y = np.triu(x, k=0)
print(y)
```

The output is as follows:

```
[[1 1 1 1 1]
 [0 1 1 1 1]
 [0 0 1 1 1]
 [0 0 0 1 1]
 [0 0 0 0 1]]
```

You can have a negative subdiagonal as follows:

```
x = np.ones((5, 5), dtype=np.uint8)
y = np.triu(x, k=-1)
print(y)
```

The output is as follows:

```
[[1 1 1 1 1]
 [1 1 1 1 1]
 [0 1 1 1 1]
 [0 0 1 1 1]
 [0 0 0 1 1]]
```

You can have a negative subdiagonal as follows:

```
x = np.ones((5, 5), dtype=np.uint8)
y = np.triu(x, k=1)
print(y)
```

The output is as follows:

```
[[0 1 1 1 1]
 [0 0 1 1 1]
 [0 0 0 1 1]
 [0 0 0 0 1]
 [0 0 0 0 0]]
```

Matplotlib

Matplotlib is an integral part of the scientific Python ecosystem, and it is used for visualization. It is an extension of NumPy. It provides a Matlab-like interface for plotting and visualization. It was originally developed by John D. Hunter as an open source alternative usable with Python.

You can install it using Jupyter Notebook as follows:

```
!pip3 install matplotlib
```

Notice the ! symbol before the `pip3` command. This is because when you want to run an OS command in a notebook, you must prefix it with !.

Before installing the Matplotlib library, you may want to upgrade pip with the following command:

```
!python -m pip install --upgrade pip
```

To use the Matplotlib library in a notebook for basic plotting, you must import its `pyplot` module as follows:

```
import matplotlib.pyplot as plt
```

The `pyplot` module provides a Matlab-like interface for creating visualizations. Also, to show the Matplotlib visualizations in the notebook, you must run the following magic command:

```
%matplotlib inline
```

This forces Matlab to show the output inline, directly below the code cell that produces the visualization. We will always use this when we need to use Matplotlib.

Let's import NumPy too as follows:

```
import numpy as np
```

You can read more about Matplotlib at `https://matplotlib.org/`.

Visualization with NumPy and Matplotlib

You are now going to learn how to create NumPy Ndarrays with Ndarray creation routines and then use Matplotlib to visualize them. Let's get started with the routines to create Ndarrays.

The first routine is `arange()`. It creates evenly spaced values with the given interval. A stop value argument is compulsory. The start value and interval parameters have the default arguments 0 and 1, respectively. Here's an example:

```
x = np.arange(6)
```

In the previous example, the stop value is 5. So, it creates an Ndarray starting with 0 and ending at 4. The function returns the sequence that has a half-open interval, which means the stop value is not included in the output. As we have not specified the interval, it assumes it to be 1. You can see the output and the datatype of it as follows:

```
print(x)
type(x)
```

The output is as follows:

```
[0 1 2 3 4 5]
numpy.ndarray
```

Let's go ahead and plot these numbers. For plotting in 2D, we need x-y pairs. Let's keep it simple and say y = f(x) = x by running the following statement:

```
y=x+1
```

Now, let's use the function plot() to visualize this. It needs the values of x and y and the plotting options. You will learn more about the plotting options later in this chapter.

```
plt.plot(x, y, 'o--')
plt.show()
```

The function show() displays the plot. As you can see, we are visualizing with plotting options o--. This means the points are represented by the solid circles and the line is dashed, as shown in Figure 3-1.

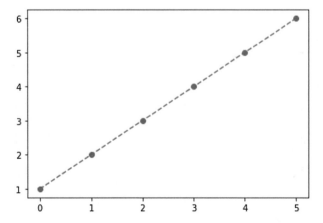

Figure 3-1. *Visualizing y=f(x)=x+1*

Here's an example of the function call for the function `arange()` with the start and stop arguments:

```
np.arange(2, 6)
```

It returns the following output (it directly prints and we are not storing it in a variable):

```
array([2, 3, 4, 5])
```

We can even add an argument for the interval as follows:

```
np.arange(2, 6, 2)
```

The output is as follows:

```
array([2, 4])
```

We can draw multiple graphs as follows:

```
plt.plot(x, y, 'o--')
plt.plot(x, -y, 'o-')
plt.show()
```

The output will have one line and another dashed line, as shown in Figure 3-2.

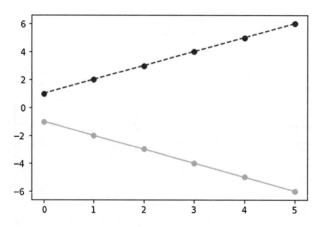

Figure 3-2. *Visualizing multiple lines*

You can even add a title to the graph as follows:

```
plt.plot(x, y, 'o--')
plt.plot(x, -y, 'o-')
plt.title('y=x and y=-x')
plt.show()
```

The output will have a title as shown in Figure 3-3.

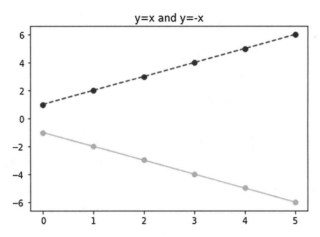

Figure 3-3. *Visualizing multiple lines and title*

The function linspace(start, stop, number) returns an array of evenly spaced numbers over a specified interval. You must pass it the starting value, the end value, and the number of values as follows:

```
N = 16
x = np.linspace(0, 15, N)
print(x)
```

The previous code creates 11 numbers (0 to 10, both inclusive) as follows:

```
[ 0.  1.  2.  3.  4.  5.  6.  7.  8.  9. 10. 11. 12. 13. 14. 15.]
```

Let's visualize this as follows:

```
y = x
plt.plot(x, y, 'o--')
plt.axis('off')
plt.show()
```

Figure 3-4 shows the output.

Figure 3-4. *Output of y = x with linspace()*

As you can see, we are turning off the axis with the line `plt.axis('off')`. Similarly, you can compute and visualize values in the logspace as follows:

```
y = np.logspace(0.1, 2, N)
print(y)
plt.plot(x, y, 'o--')
plt.show()
```

The output of the print function is as follows:

```
[   1.25892541   1.68525904    2.25597007    3.01995172    4.04265487
     5.41169527   7.2443596     9.69765359   12.98175275   17.37800829
    23.26305067  31.14105584   41.68693835   55.80417175   74.70218989
   100.           ]
```

Figure 3-5 shows the output.

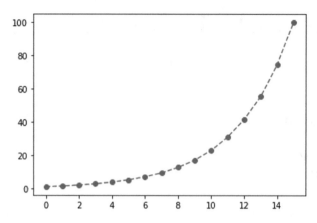

Figure 3-5. *Output of logspace()*

You can even compute a series in the geometric progression as follows:

```
y = np.geomspace(0.1, 2000, N)
print(y)
plt.plot(x, y, 'o--')
plt.show()
```

The output of the print statement is as follows:

```
[1.00000000e-01 1.93524223e-01 3.74516250e-01 7.24779664e-01
 1.40262421e+00 2.71441762e+00 5.25305561e+00 1.01659351e+01
 1.96735469e+01 3.80730788e+01 7.36806300e+01 1.42589867e+02
 2.75945932e+02 5.34022222e+02 1.03346236e+03 2.00000000e+03]
```

Figure 3-6 shows the output.

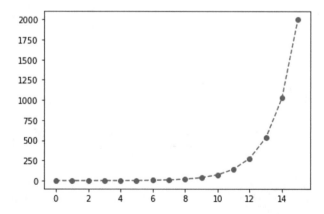

Figure 3-6. *Output of geomspace()*

Running the Matplotlib Program as a Script

You can use Python's script mode to run the Matplotlib program. Save the program shown in Listing 3-1 as prog01.py.

Listing 3-1. prog01.py

```
import numpy as np
import matplotlib.pyplot as plt

x = np.arange(6)
print(x)
type(x)

y=x+1

plt.plot(x, y, 'o--')
plt.show()
```

When you run this program, the output is shown in a separate window, as shown in Figure 3-7.

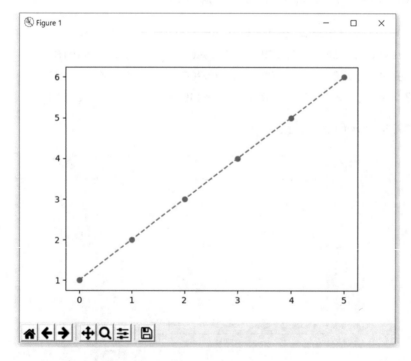

Figure 3-7. *Output in a separate window*

We will mostly be using Jupyter Notebook to show the visualizations in the browser window.

Summary

This chapter focused on the routines for creating Ndarrays. You also learned the basics of Matplotlib. Along with the basics, you learned how to visualize Ndarrays with simple graphs. There is more to NumPy and Matplotlib than what you learned in this chapter. There are many more NumPy and data visualization routines.

In the next chapter, you will explore more such NumPy routines that manipulate NumPy Ndarrays.

CHAPTER 4

Revisiting Matplotlib Visualizations

In the previous chapter, you learned about the many routines for creating and manipulating Ndarrays in the NumPy library. You will need many of those routines throughout this book.

This chapter is dedicated to exploring the aesthetic aspects of visualizations prepared with Matplotlib. You will learn to customize the cosmetic aspects of the Matplotlib visualizations. Specifically, we will explore the following topics in detail:

- Single-line plots

- Multiline plots

- Grid, axes, and labels

- Colors, lines, and markers

- Subplots

- Object-oriented style

- Working with the text

After reading this chapter, you will be able to programmatically customize the aesthetic aspects of your visualizations to make them more presentable.

Single-Line Plots

When there is only one visualization in a figure that uses the function `plot()`, then it is known as a *single-line plot*. In this section, you'll see a few ways that you can draw a single-line plot. We have already used the function `plot()` to draw single-line plots. Let's explore this concept further in detail with a few more solid examples.

© Ashwin Pajankar 2022
A. Pajankar, *Hands-on Matplotlib*, https://doi.org/10.1007/978-1-4842-7410-1_4

Create a new notebook for the demonstrations in this chapter. You can also use Python lists to visualize the plots, as follows:

```
%matplotlib inline
import matplotlib.pyplot as plt
x = [4, 5, 3, 1, 6, 7]
plt.plot(x)
plt.show()
```

Figure 4-1 shows the output.

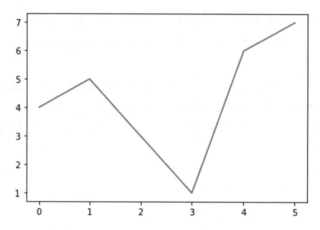

Figure 4-1. *Demonstrating a simple single-line graph*

In this case, the values of the y-axis are assumed.

Here's another example of a single-line graph that uses an Ndarray:

```
import numpy as np
x = np.arange(25)
plt.plot(x)
plt.show()
```

Figure 4-2 shows the output.

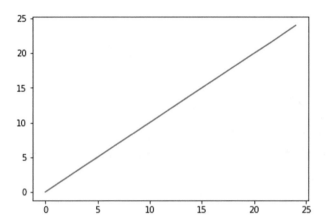

Figure 4-2. *A simple single-line graph with arange()*

Let's visualize the quadratic graph y = f(x) = x³+1. The code is as follows:

```
plt.plot(x, [(y**3 + 1) for y in x])
plt.show()
```

Figure 4-3 shows the output.

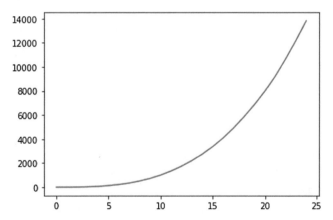

Figure 4-3. $y = f(x) = x^3 + 1$

You can write the same code in a simple way as follows:

```
plt.plot(x, x**3 + 1)
plt.show()
```

Multiline Plots

It is possible to visualize multiple plots in the same output. Let's see how to show multiple curves in the same visualization. The following is a simple example:

```
%matplotlib inline
import numpy as np
import matplotlib.pyplot as plt
x = np.arange(7)
plt.plot(x, -x**2)
plt.plot(x, -x**3)
plt.plot(x, -2*x)
plt.plot(x, -2**x)
plt.show()
```

Figure 4-4 shows the output.

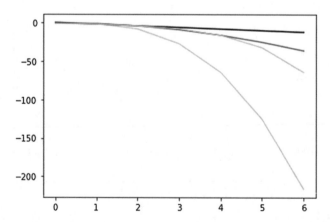

Figure 4-4. *Multiline graph*

As you can see, Matplotlib automatically assigns colors to the curves separately.

You can write the same code in a simple way as follows:

```
plt.plot(x, -x**2, x, -x**3,
        x, -2*x, x, -2**x)
plt.show()
```

The output will be the same as Figure 4-4.

Let's see another example:

```
x = np.array([[3, 2, 5, 6], [7, 4, 1, 5]])
plt.plot(x)
plt.show()
```

Figure 4-5 shows the output.

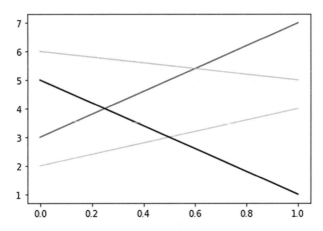

Figure 4-5. *Multiline graph, another example*

You can also create a multiline graph with random data as follows:

```
data = np.random.randn(2, 10)
print(data)
plt.plot([data[0], data[1]])
plt.show()
```

Figure 4-6 shows the output.

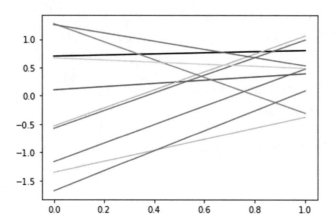

Figure 4-6. *Multiline graph, random data*

In this example, we generated the data in a random way using the routine `np.random.randn()`. Since this routine will generate the random data, the output will be different every time we execute it. So, the output you will see will be different every time you execute the code.

Grid, Axes, and Labels

Now you will learn how to enable a grid in the visualizations. This can be done with the statement `plt.grid(True)`. You will also learn how to manipulate the limits of axes. But before that, you will quickly learn how to save a visualization as an image on the hard disk. Look at the following code:

```
x = np.arange(3)
plt.plot(x, -x**2, x, -x**3, x, -2*x, x, -2**x)
plt.grid(True)
plt.savefig('test.png')
plt.show()
```

The statement `plt.savefig('test.png')` saves the image in the current directory of the Jupyter Notebook file. Figure 4-7 shows the output.

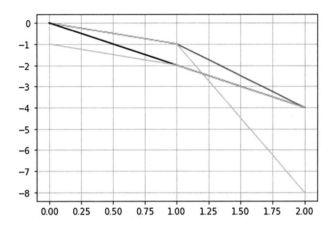

Figure 4-7. *Multiline graph*

You can see that the limits of the axes are set by default as follows:

```
x = np.arange(3)
plt.plot(x, -x**2, x, -x**3, x, -2*x, x, -2**x)
plt.grid(True)
print(plt.axis())
plt.show()
```

Figure 4-8 shows the output.

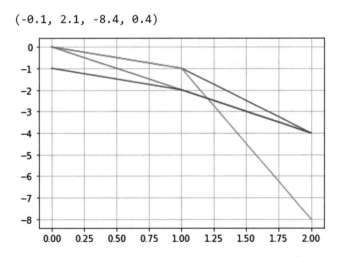

Figure 4-8. *Seeing the values of axes*

You can also customize the values of the axes as follows:

```
x = np.arange(3)
plt.plot(x, -x**2, x, -x**3, x, -2*x, x, -2**x)
plt.grid(True)
plt.axis([0, 2, -8, 0])
print(plt.axis())
plt.show()
```

The statement plt.axis([0, 2, -8, 0]) sets the values of the axes. The first pair, (0, 2), refers to the limits for the x-axis, and the second pair, (-8, 0), refers to the limits for the y-axis. You can write the previous code with different syntax using the functions xlim() and ylim() as follows:

```
x = np.arange(3)
plt.plot(x, -x**2, x, -x**3, x, -2*x, x, -2**x)
plt.grid(True)
plt.xlim([0, 2])
plt.ylim([-8, 0])
print(plt.axis())
plt.show()
```

Both the examples produce the same output, as shown in Figure 4-9.

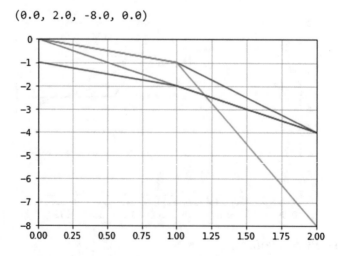

Figure 4-9. *Customizing the axes*

You can add the title and the labels for the axes as follows:

```
x = np.arange(3)
plt.plot(x, -x**2, x, -x**3, x, -2*x, x, -2**x)
plt.grid(True)
plt.xlabel('x = np.arange(3)')
plt.xlim([0, 2])
plt.ylabel('y = f(x)')
plt.ylim([-8, 0])
plt.title('Simple Plot Demo')
plt.show()
```

This produces output with the labels and the title shown in Figure 4-10.

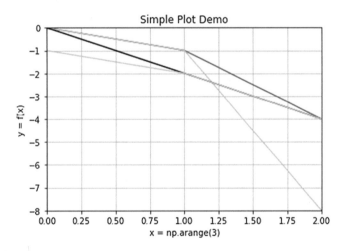

Figure 4-10. *Title for the visualization and labels for the axes*

You can pass an argument for the parameter label in the plot() function and then call the function legend() to create a legend as follows:

```
x = np.arange(3)
plt.plot(x, -x**2, label='-x**2')
plt.plot(x, -x**3, label='-x**3')
plt.plot(x, -2*x, label='-2*x')
plt.plot(x, -2**x, label='-2**x')
plt.legend()
```

```
plt.grid(True)
plt.xlabel('x = np.arange(3)')
plt.xlim([0, 2])
plt.ylabel('y = f(x)')
plt.ylim([-8, 0])
plt.title('Simple Plot Demo')
plt.show()
```

This code produces output with legends for the curves, as shown in Figure 4-11.

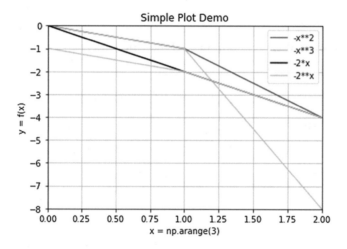

Figure 4-11. *Output with legends*

Instead of passing the legend string as an argument to the function plot(), you can pass the list of strings as an argument to the function legend() as follows:

```
x = np.arange(3)
plt.plot(x, -x**2, x, -x**3, x, -2*x, x, -2**x)
plt.legend(['-x**2', '-x**3', '-2*x', '-2**x'])
plt.grid(True)
plt.xlabel('x = np.arange(3)')
plt.xlim([0, 2])
plt.ylabel('y = f(x)')
plt.ylim([-8, 0])
plt.title('Simple Plot Demo')
plt.show()
```

This produces the same output as Figure 4-11.

You can also change the location of the legend box by making the following changes to `plt.legend()` from the previous code:

```
x = np.arange(3)
plt.plot(x, -x**2, x, -x**3, x, -2*x, x, -2**x)
plt.legend(['-x**2', '-x**3', '-2*x', '-2**x'],
           loc='lower center')
plt.grid(True)
plt.xlabel('x = np.arange(3)')
plt.xlim([0, 2])
plt.ylabel('y = f(x)')
plt.ylim([-8, 0])
plt.title('Simple Plot Demo')
plt.show()
```

Figure 4-12 shows the output.

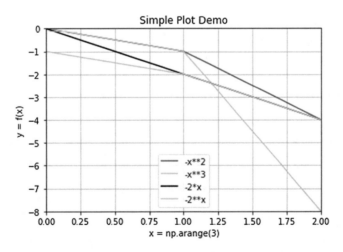

Figure 4-12. *Output with legends in upper middle position*

Finally, let's save the visualization to disk with the following code:

```
x = np.arange(3)
plt.plot(x, -x**2, x, -x**3, x, -2*x, x, -2**x)
plt.legend(['-x**2', '-x**3', '-2*x', '-2**x'],
           loc='lower center')
```

```
plt.grid(True)
plt.xlabel('x = np.arange(3)')
plt.xlim([0, 2])
plt.ylabel('y = f(x)')
plt.ylim([-8, 0])
plt.title('Simple Plot Demo')
plt.savefig('test.png')
plt.show()
```

Colors, Styles, and Markers

Up until now, in the case of multiline plots, you have seen that Matplotlib automatically assigned colors, styles, and markers. You saw a few examples of how to customize them. Now, in this section, you will learn how to customize them in detail.

Let's start with colors. The following code lists all the primary colors supported by Matplotlib (we are not customizing styles and markers in this example):

```
%matplotlib inline
import matplotlib.pyplot as plt
import numpy as np

x = np.arange(5)
y = x
plt.plot(x, y+0.4, 'g')
plt.plot(x, y+0.2, 'y')
plt.plot(x, y, 'r')
plt.plot(x, y-0.2, 'c')
plt.plot(x, y-0.4, 'k')
plt.plot(x, y-0.6, 'm')
plt.plot(x, y-0.8, 'w')
plt.plot(x, y-1, 'b')
plt.show()
```

Figure 4-13 shows the output.

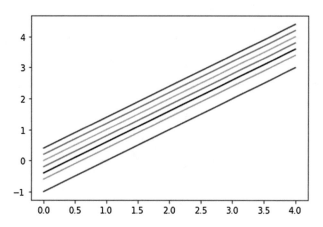

Figure 4-13. *Demo of colors*

You can also write the previous code as follows:

```
plt.plot(x, y+0.4, 'g', x, y+0.2, 'y', x, y, 'r', x, y-0.2, 'c', x, y-0.4,
'k', x, y-0.6, 'm', x, y-0.8, 'w', x, y-1, 'b')
plt.show()
```

The output will be the same as Figure 4-13.
You can customize the line style as follows:

```
plt.plot(x, y, '-', x, y+1, '--', x, y+2, '-.', x, y+3, ':')
plt.show()
```

Figure 4-14 shows the output.

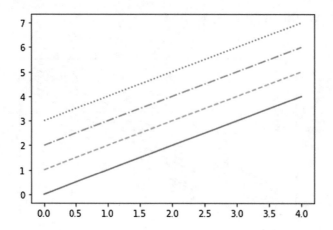

Figure 4-14. *Line styles*

You can even change the markers as follows:

```
plt.plot(x, y, '.')
plt.plot(x, y+0.5, ',')
plt.plot(x, y+1, 'o')
plt.plot(x, y+2, '<')
plt.plot(x, y+3, '>')
plt.plot(x, y+4, 'v')
plt.plot(x, y+5, '^')
plt.plot(x, y+6, '1')
plt.plot(x, y+7, '2')
plt.plot(x, y+8, '3')
plt.plot(x, y+9, '4')
plt.plot(x, y+10, 's')
plt.plot(x, y+11, 'p')
plt.plot(x, y+12, '*')
plt.plot(x, y+13, 'h')
plt.plot(x, y+14, 'H')
plt.plot(x, y+15, '+')
plt.plot(x, y+16, 'D')
plt.plot(x, y+17, 'd')
plt.plot(x, y+18, '|')
plt.plot(x, y+19, '_')
plt.show()
```

Figure 4-15 shows the output.

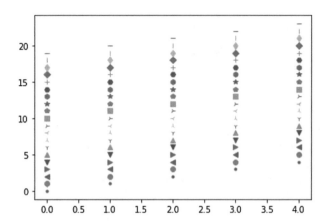

Figure 4-15. *Markers*

You can combine all three techniques (for colors, markers, and line styles) to customize the visualization as follows:

```
plt.plot(x, y, 'mo--')
plt.plot(x, y+1 , 'g*-.')
plt.show()
```

Figure 4-16 shows the output.

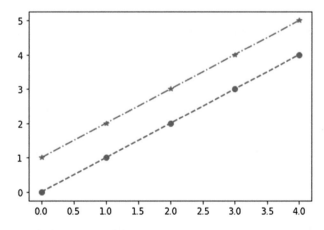

Figure 4-16. *Customizing everything*

These are the basic customizations you can do in Matplotlib. You can customize everything in great detail. Here is a code example:

```
plt.plot(x, y, color='g', linestyle='--', linewidth=1.5,
        marker='^', markerfacecolor='b', markeredgecolor='k',
        markeredgewidth=1.5, markersize=5)
plt.grid(True)
plt.show()
```

Figure 4-17 shows the output.

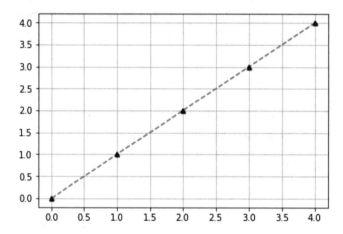

Figure 4-17. *Customizing everything in greater detail*

You can even customize the values on the x- and y-axes as follows:

```
x = y = np.arange(10)
plt.plot(x, y, 'o--')
plt.xticks(range(len(x)), ['a', 'b', 'c', 'd', 'e', 'f', 'g', 'h', 'i', 'j'])
plt.yticks(range(0, 10, 1))
plt.show()
```

Figure 4-18 shows the output.

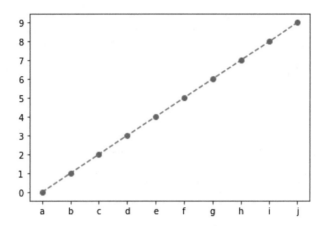

Figure 4-18. *Customizing the ticks on the axes*

Object-Oriented Plotting

You can create plots in an object-oriented way. Let's rewrite one of our earlier code examples as follows:

```
fig, ax = plt.subplots()
ax.plot(x, -x**2, label='-x**2')
ax.plot(x, -x**3, label='-x**3')
ax.plot(x, -2*x, label='-2*x')
ax.plot(x, -2**x, label='-2**x')
ax.set_xlabel('x = np.arange(3)')
ax.set_ylabel('y = f(x)')
ax.set_title('Simple Plot Demo')
ax.legend()
ax.grid(True)
plt.show()
```

Note that we are using the axis object to plot and set the labels and a title. Figure 4-19 shows the output.

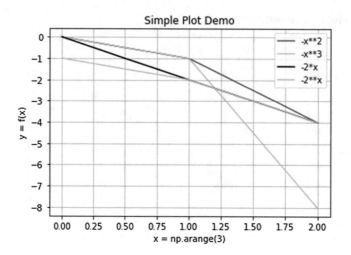

Figure 4-19. *Output of object-oriented plotting*

You can also add the text with the functions `ax.text()` or the function `plt.text()`. The functions accept the coordinates and the text to be displayed. The following is an example:

```
fig, ax = plt.subplots()
ax.plot(x, -x**2, label='-x**2')
ax.plot(x, -x**3, label='-x**3')
ax.plot(x, -2*x, label='-2*x')
ax.plot(x, -2**x, label='-2**x')
ax.set_xlabel('x = np.arange(3)')
ax.set_ylabel('y = f(x)')
ax.set_title('Simple Plot Demo')
ax.legend()
ax.grid(True)
ax.text(0.25, -5, "Simple Plot Demo")
plt.show()
```

Figure 4-20 shows the output.

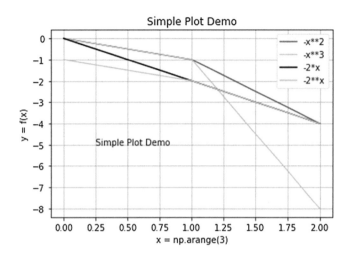

Figure 4-20. *Rendering text*

Subplots

You can show multiple separate graphs in the same output. The technique is known as *subplotting*. Subplots can have their own titles, own labels, and other specifications. Subplots are created in a grid. The first subplot position is at the top left. The other subplot positions are relative to the first position. The following is an example:

```
x = np.arange(3)
plt.subplots_adjust(wspace=0.3,
                    hspace=0.3)
plt.subplot(2, 2, 1)
plt.plot(x, -x**2)
plt.subplot(2, 2, 2)
plt.plot(x, -x**3)
plt.subplot(2, 2, 3)
plt.plot(x, -2*x)
plt.subplot(2, 2, 4)
plt.plot(x, -2**x)
plt.show()
```

The first two arguments passed to `plt.subplot()` represent the grid size, and the third argument indicates the position of that particular subplot. Figure 4-21 shows the output.

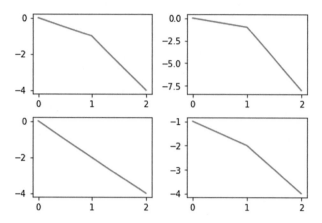

Figure 4-21. *Subplots*

You can write the same code in object-oriented fashion as follows:

```
fig, axs = plt.subplots(2, 2)
plt.subplots_adjust(wspace=0.3,
                    hspace=0.3)
axs[0, 0].plot(x, -x**2)
axs[0, 1].plot(x, -x**3)
axs[1, 0].plot(x, -2*x)
axs[1, 1].plot(x, -2**x)
plt.show()
```

The code produces the same output as shown in Figure 4-21.

Summary

This chapter focused on visualizations and various customizations. You learned a great deal about visualizing the data and customizing the visualizations as per the requirements. You also learned about the object-oriented style of plotting and subplots. The concepts you learned in this chapter will be used throughout this book to visualize the data.

In the next chapter, we will explore more stylesheets, legends, and layout computations.

CHAPTER 5

Styles and Layouts

In the previous chapter, you learned about many advanced concepts related to creating visualizations with Matplotlib.

We will continue exploring more concepts related to visualization in greater detail in this chapter. Specifically, we will explore the following topics in detail:

- Styles

- Layouts

After reading this chapter, you will be able to work with colors, stylesheets, and custom layouts.

Styles

In this section, you will explore the various styles available in Matplotlib. Up until now we have been working with the default style. A style dictates things such as marker size, colors, and fonts. There are many built-in styles in Matplotlib. The following is a short example of applying a built-in style:

```
%matplotlib inline
import matplotlib.pyplot as plt
import numpy as np
plt.style.use('ggplot')
data = np.random.randn(10)
```

Let's visualize it now:

```
plt.plot(data)
plt.show()
```

© Ashwin Pajankar 2022
A. Pajankar, *Hands-on Matplotlib*, https://doi.org/10.1007/978-1-4842-7410-1_5

Here we are using the style of ggplot2, which is a visualization package for the R programming language. Figure 5-1 shows the output.

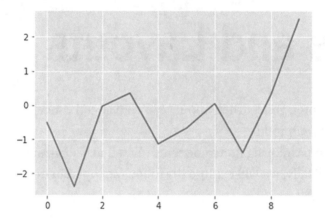

Figure 5-1. *ggplot style*

You must be curious to know the names of all the available styles. You can print the names using this:

```
print(plt.style.available)
```

The following is the output that shows the name of all the available styles:

```
['Solarize_Light2', '_classic_test_patch', 'bmh', 'classic', 'dark_
background', 'fast', 'fivethirtyeight', 'ggplot', 'grayscale', 'seaborn',
'seaborn-bright', 'seaborn-colorblind', 'seaborn-dark', 'seaborn-
dark-palette', 'seaborn-darkgrid', 'seaborn-deep', 'seaborn-muted',
'seaborn-notebook', 'seaborn-paper', 'seaborn-pastel', 'seaborn-poster',
'seaborn-talk', 'seaborn-ticks', 'seaborn-white', 'seaborn-whitegrid',
'tableau-colorblind10']
```

Let's apply the classic `matplotlib` style as follows:

```
plt.style.use('classic')
plt.plot(data)
plt.show()
```

Figure 5-2 shows the output.

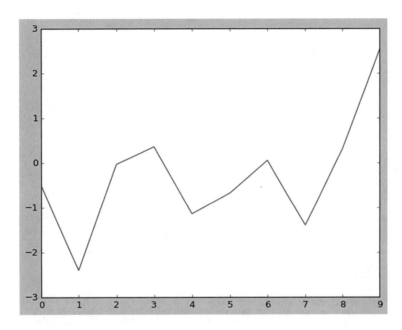

Figure 5-2. *Classic style*

Note that once you apply a style, that style applies to the entire notebook. So, if you want to switch back to the default style, you can use the following code:

```
plt.style.use('default')
```

Let's show the data with the following:

```
plt.plot(data)
plt.show()
```

Figure 5-3 shows the output.

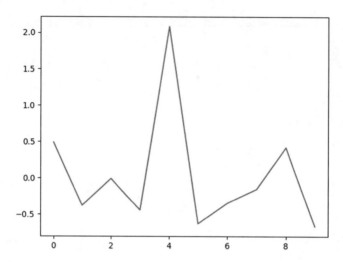

Figure 5-3. *Default style*

Now let's demonstrate how the colors are affected when we change the styles. Let's define the data as shown here:

```
n = 3
data = np.linspace(0, 2*n*np.pi, 300)
```

In addition, let's define a custom function as follows:

```
def sinusoidal(sty):
    plt.style.use(sty)
    fig, ax = plt.subplots()

    ax.plot(data, np.sin(data), label='Sine')
    ax.plot(data, np.cos(data), label='Cosine')
    ax.legend()
```

A function is a routine that can be called to perform some operation. Until now, we have been using library functions that come with Python itself and libraries like NumPy and Matplotlib. Here, in the code snippet, we have defined our own custom function.

This custom function accepts an argument. We are using the passed argument as a style for our visualization. Let's call this function with the default styling, as shown here:

```
sinusoidal('default')
plt.show()
```

Figure 5-4 shows the output.

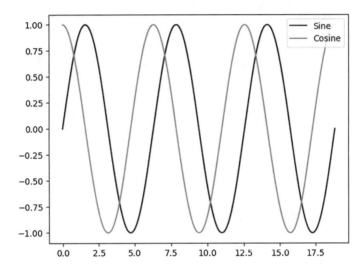

Figure 5-4. *Default style sinusoidal graph*

Let's use the ggplot style as follows:

```
sinusoidal('ggplot')
plt.show()
```

Figure 5-5 shows the output.

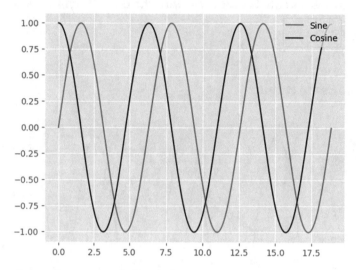

Figure 5-5. *ggplot-style sinusoidal graph*

Let's see the Seaborn style, as shown here:

```
sinusoidal('seaborn')
plt.show()
```

Figure 5-6 shows the output.

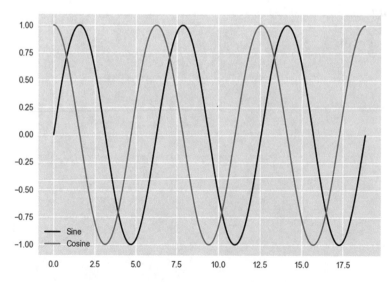

Figure 5-6. *Seaborn-style sinusoidal graph*

You have seen that the styling is applied globally to the entire notebook, and you have learned to switch to the default styling. You can locally change the styling for a block of code as follows:

```
with plt.style.context('Solarize_Light2'):
    data = np.linspace(0, 6 * np.pi)
    plt.plot(np.sin(data), 'g.--')
    plt.show()
```

Figure 5-7 shows the output.

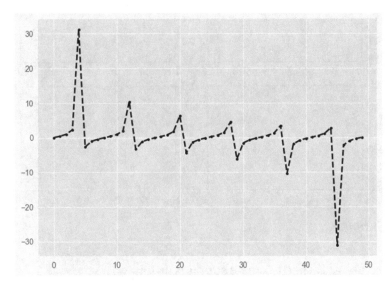

Figure 5-7. *Temporary styling*

Layouts

In this section, you will study layouts. You already learned about subplots in Chapter 4, and if you want to use the default style again, you can run the following line of code to reset the styling to the default style:

```
plt.style.use('default')
```

Let's revise that and create a 2×2 visualization as follows:

```
fig, axs = plt.subplots(ncols=2, nrows=2,
                        constrained_layout=True)
plt.show()
```

Figure 5-8 shows the output.

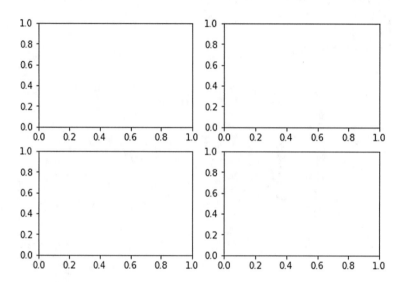

Figure 5-8. *Subplots*

You can also use `gridspec` to create subplots as follows:

```
import matplotlib.gridspec as gridspec

fig = plt.figure(constrained_layout=True)
specs = gridspec.GridSpec(ncols=2, nrows=2, figure=fig)
ax1 = fig.add_subplot(specs[0, 0])
ax2 = fig.add_subplot(specs[0, 1])
ax3 = fig.add_subplot(specs[1, 0])
ax4 = fig.add_subplot(specs[1, 1])
plt.show()
```

The previous code will create a subplot that looks like Figure 5-8. You have to write a lot of code for the output that can be obtained in just a couple of lines of code. However, you can use this method to create more complex visualizations. Let's create a 3×3 visualization such that an entire row is occupied by a plot.

```
fig = plt.figure(constrained_layout=True)
gs = fig.add_gridspec(3, 3)
ax1 = fig.add_subplot(gs[0, :])
ax1.set_title('gs[0, :]')
ax2 = fig.add_subplot(gs[1, :])
ax2.set_title('gs[1, :]')
ax3 = fig.add_subplot(gs[2, :])
ax3.set_title('gs[2, :]')
plt.show()
```

This code will produce the output shown in Figure 5-9.

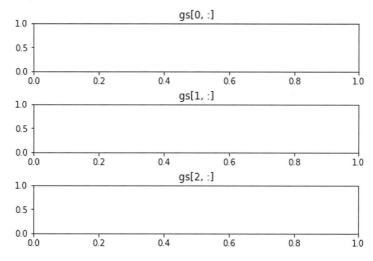

Figure 5-9. *Customized subplots*

You can also have vertical plots as follows:

```
fig = plt.figure(constrained_layout=True)
gs = fig.add_gridspec(3, 3)
ax1 = fig.add_subplot(gs[:, 0])
ax1.set_title('gs[:, 0]')
ax2 = fig.add_subplot(gs[:, 1])
ax2.set_title('gs[:, 1]')
ax3 = fig.add_subplot(gs[:, 2])
ax3.set_title('gs[:, 2]')
plt.show()
```

Figure 5-10 shows the output.

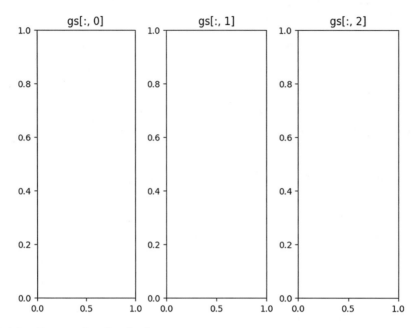

Figure 5-10. *Customized subplots*

Let's see a more complex example.

```
fig = plt.figure(constrained_layout=True)
gs = fig.add_gridspec(3, 3)
ax1 = fig.add_subplot(gs[0, :])
ax1.set_title('gs[0, :]')
ax2 = fig.add_subplot(gs[1, :-1])
ax2.set_title('gs[1, :-1]')
ax3 = fig.add_subplot(gs[1:, -1])
ax3.set_title('gs[1:, -1]')
ax4 = fig.add_subplot(gs[-1, 0])
ax4.set_title('gs[-1, 0]')
ax5 = fig.add_subplot(gs[-1, -2])
ax5.set_title('gs[-1, -2]')
plt.show()
```

Figure 5-11 shows the output.

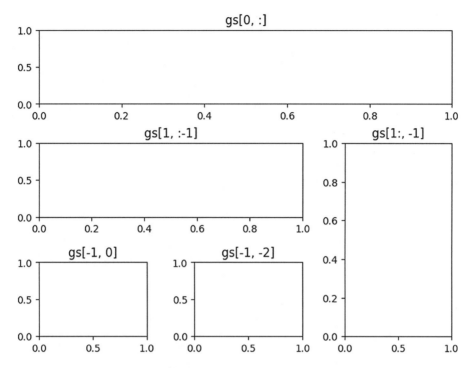

Figure 5-11. *Customized subplots*

This is how you can customize subplots.

Summary

This chapter focused on the styles and subplots. You will be using these concepts sparingly throughout the book.

In the next chapter, we will explore a few recipes of Matplotlib to create visualizations.

CHAPTER 6

Lines, Bars, and Scatter Plots

In the previous chapter, you learned about many advanced concepts related to visualizations with Matplotlib.

In this chapter and the next few chapters, you will learn some techniques for creating data visualizations. Specifically, in this chapter, you will learn how to create the following data visualizations:

- Lines and logs

- Error bars

- Bar graphs

- Scatter plots

After reading this chapter, you will be able to work with lines, logs, bars, and scatter plots.

Lines and Logs

You already saw how to plot lines in an earlier chapter. Just to warm up, let's look at an example of a line again, as shown here:

```
%matplotlib inline
import numpy as np
import matplotlib.pyplot as plt
data = np.linspace(0, 9, 10)
```

© Ashwin Pajankar 2022
A. Pajankar, *Hands-on Matplotlib*, https://doi.org/10.1007/978-1-4842-7410-1_6

Let's visualize it now.

```
plt.plot(data)
plt.show()
```

Figure 6-1 shows the output.

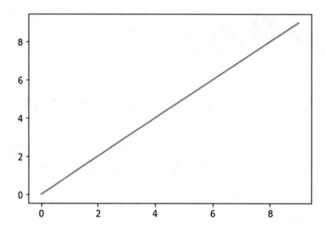

Figure 6-1. *Line plot example*

Let's create a graph such that the x-axis is logarithmic and the y-axis is normal, as shown here:

```
t = np.arange(0.01, 10, 0.01)
plt.semilogx(t, np.cos(2 * np.pi * t))
plt.show()
```

Figure 6-2 shows the output.

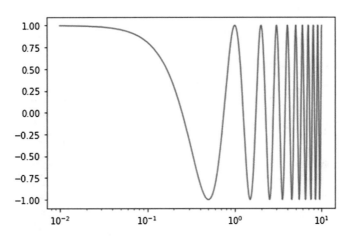

Figure 6-2. *Normal y-axis and logarithmic x-axis*

Similarly, you can create a logarithmic y-axis and a normal x-axis as follows:

```
plt.semilogy(t, np.cos(2 * np.pi * t))
plt.show()
```

Figure 6-3 shows the output.

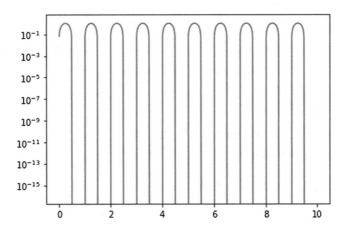

Figure 6-3. *Normal x-axis and logarithmic y-axis*

You can have both axes be logarithmic, as shown here:

```
plt.loglog(t, np.cos(2 * np.pi * t))
plt.show()
```

Figure 6-4 shows the output.

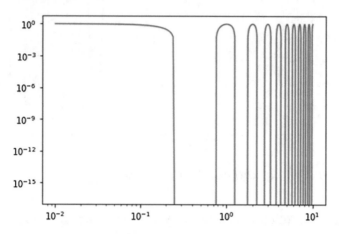

Figure 6-4. *Both logarithmic axes*

Error Bars

You can also use visualizations to show error in data. When there is a possibility of errors in the observed data, you usually want to mention it in the observation. You would say something like "there's a 96 percent confidence interval." This means that there is a possibility of 4 percent error in the given data. This gives people a general idea about the precision of the quantity. When you want to represent this confidence (or lack thereof), you can use error bars.

You have to use the function errorbar() for this. You can create an Ndarray or list to store the error data. We can either have real-life data or simulate it as follows:

```
x = np.linspace (0, 2 * np.pi, 100)
y = np.sin(x)
ye = np.random.rand(len(x))/10
plt.errorbar(x, y, yerr = ye)
plt.show()
```

In this example, we are showing the error on the y-axis. Figure 6-5 shows the output.

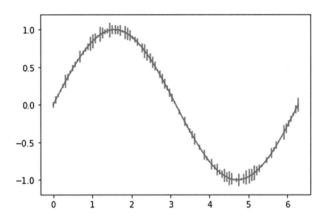

Figure 6-5. *Error on the y-axis*

Similarly, you can show the error data on the x-axis.

```
xe = np.random.rand(len(x))/10
plt.errorbar(x, y, xerr = xe)
plt.show()
```

Figure 6-6 shows the output.

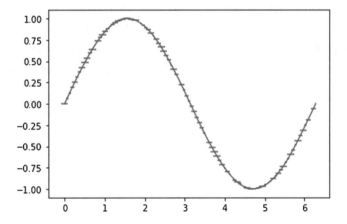

Figure 6-6. *Error on the x-axis*

You can show errors on both axes as follows:

```
plt.errorbar(x, y, xerr = xe, yerr = ye)
plt.show()
```

Figure 6-7 shows the output.

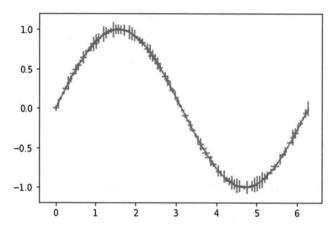

Figure 6-7. *Error on both axes*

Bar Graphs

A bar graph is a representation of discrete and categorical data items with bars. You can represent the data with vertical or horizontal bars. The height or length of bars is always in proportion to the magnitude of the data. You can use bar charts or bar graphs when you have discrete categorical data. The following is a simple example of a bar graph:

```
x = np.arange(4)
y = np.random.rand(4)
plt.bar(x, y)
plt.show()
```

Figure 6-8 shows the output.

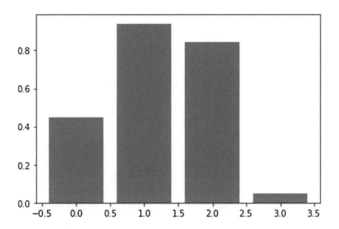

Figure 6-8. *Bar graph*

You can have a combined bar graph as follows:

```
y = np.random.rand(3, 4)
plt.bar(x + 0.00, y[0], color = 'b', width = 0.25)
plt.bar(x + 0.25, y[1], color = 'g', width = 0.25)
plt.bar(x + 0.50, y[2], color = 'r', width = 0.25)
plt.show()
```

Figure 6-9 shows the output.

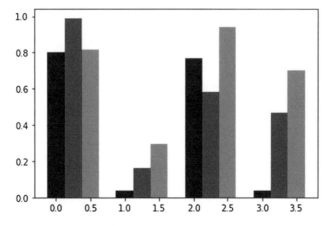

Figure 6-9. *Combined bar graph*

The previous graphs were examples of vertical bar graphs. Similarly, you can have horizontal bar graphs as follows:

```
x = np.arange(4)
y = np.random.rand(4)
plt.barh(x, y)
plt.show()
```

Figure 6-10 shows the output.

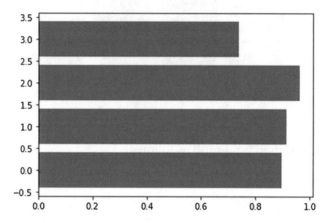

Figure 6-10. *Horizontal bar graph*

You can also have combined horizontal bar graphs as follows:

```
y = np.random.rand(3, 4)
plt.barh(x + 0.00, y[0], color = 'b', height=0.25)
plt.barh(x + 0.25, y[1], color = 'g', height=0.25)
plt.barh(x + 0.50, y[2], color = 'r', height=0.25)
plt.show()
```

Figure 6-11 shows the output.

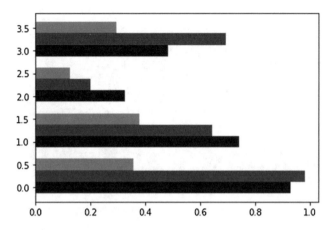

Figure 6-11. *Combined horizontal bar graph*

Scatter Plot

You can also visualize your data with scatter plots. You will usually visualize a set of two variables with a scatter plot. One variable is assigned to the x-axis, and another is assigned to the y-axis. Then you draw a point for the values of x-y pairs. The size of x and y must be same (they are always one-dimensional arrays). You can show additional variables by manipulating the colors and sizes of the points. In that case, the sizes of the one-dimensional arrays representing x, y, the color, and the size must be the same.

In the following example, we are assigning random x- and y-axes values and colors to 1,000 points. All points are of size 20.

```
N = 1000
x = np.random.rand(N)
y = np.random.rand(N)
colors = np.random.rand(N)
size = (20)
plt.scatter(x, y, s=size, c=colors, alpha=1)
plt.show()
```

Figure 6-12 shows the output.

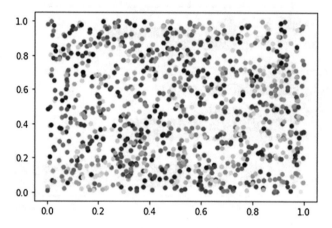

Figure 6-12. *Scatter plot*

The size of the points is fixed in this example. You can also set the size per the place on the graph (which depends on the values of the x and y coordinates). Here is an example:

```
N = 1000
x = np.random.rand(N)
y = np.random.rand(N)
colors = np.random.rand(N)
size = (50 * x * y)
plt.scatter(x, y, s=size, c=colors, alpha=1)
plt.show()
```

Figure 6-13 shows the output.

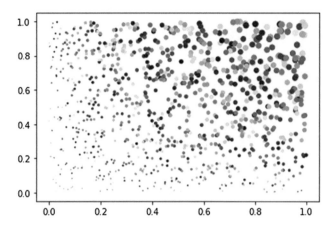

Figure 6-13. *Scatter plot*

You've just learned how to create scatter plots.

Summary

In this chapter, we started with a little bit of a warm-up with a line plot. You then learned how to create various log graphs. You also learned how to show the margin of error and how to create bar plots. Finally, you learned how to create scatter plots.

In the next chapter, you will learn a few more techniques for creating data visualizations. You will learn how to create histograms, contours, stream plots, and heatmaps.

CHAPTER 7

Histograms, Contours, and Stream Plots

In the previous chapter, you learned many ways to create visualizations with lines, bar plots, and scatter plots.

We will continue exploring various visualizations with Matplotlib in this chapter. You will learn how to create histograms and contours. You will also learn how to plot vectors with stream plots.

Histograms

Before you learn how to create various types of histograms, you need to learn what they are. First, you need to know what frequency tables are. Suppose you have a set of members with various values. You can create a table that has various buckets of ranges of values in a column. Each bucket must have at least one value. Then you can count the number of members that fall into that bucket and note those counts against the buckets. Let's see a simple example. Please create a new notebook for this, as shown here:

```
%matplotlib inline
import numpy as np
import matplotlib.pyplot as plt
```

Now let's manually create a dataset and define the number of buckets equal to the cardinality (number of distinct elements) of the set.

```
x = [1, 3, 5, 1, 2, 4, 4, 2, 5, 4, 3, 1, 2]
n_bins = 5
```

© Ashwin Pajankar 2022
A. Pajankar, *Hands-on Matplotlib*, https://doi.org/10.1007/978-1-4842-7410-1_7

You can show the output with the following code:

```
plt.hist(x, bins=n_bins)
plt.show()
```

Figure 7-1 shows the output.

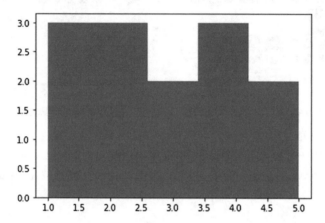

Figure 7-1. *Simple histogram*

Normal (or Gaussian) distribution is a type of continuous probability distribution. It is usually a bell-shaped curve. Let's create a histogram with a normal distribution curve. To create the data, we will use a NumPy routine. Let's draw a histogram of random data with normal distribution as follows:

```
np.random.seed(31415)
n_points = 10000
n_bins = 15
x = np.random.randn(n_points)
plt.hist(x, bins=n_bins)
plt.show()
```

Figure 7-2 shows the output.

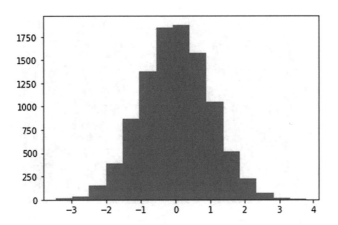

Figure 7-2. *Simple histogram of random data*

The histogram of one-dimensional data is a 2D figure (as shown in Figure 7-2). When you want to create a histogram of 2D data, you have to create a 3D figure with the data variables on the x- and y-axes and the histogram on the z-axis. In other words, you can use 2D coordinates to show this 3D visualization and view the histogram from the top (top view). The bars can be color coded to signify their magnitude.

```
y = np.random.randn(n_points)
plt.hist2d(x, y, bins=50)
plt.show()
```

Figure 7-3 shows the output.

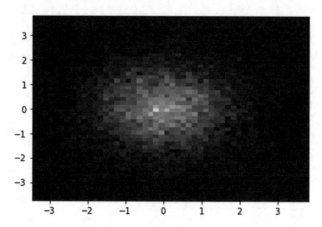

Figure 7-3. *Simple histogram of 2D data*

You can customize the histogram by setting the transparency and the color as follows:

```
plt.hist(x, 20, density=True,
        histtype='stepfilled',
        facecolor='g', alpha=0.5)
plt.show()
```

Figure 7-4 shows the output.

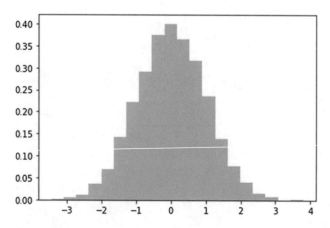

Figure 7-4. *Customized histogram*

You can also show just the outline of the histogram as follows:

```
plt.hist(x, 20, density=True,
         histtype='step')
plt.show()
```

Figure 7-5 shows the output.

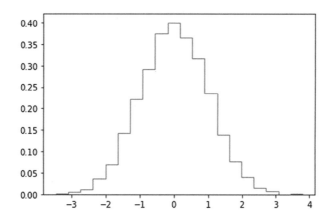

Figure 7-5. *Customized histogram with outline only*

Contours

Contours represent the outline of an object. Contours are continuous (and closed, in many cases) lines highlighting the shape of objects. Contours are useful in the area of cartography, which means map-making. On maps, a contour joins points of equal height. So, all the points on a contour line are at an equal elevation (from the sea level). In other applications where we use contours, all the points on the same contour line have the same values (or magnitude).

Let's draw a simple contour. We will create and visualize our own data by creating circular contour as follows:

```
x = np.arange(-3, 3, 0.005)
y = np.arange(-3, 3, 0.005)
X, Y = np.meshgrid(x, y)
Z = (X**2 + Y**2)
```

```
out = plt.contour(X, Y, Z)
plt.clabel(out, inline=True,
           fontsize=10)
plt.show()
```

Figure 7-6 shows the output.

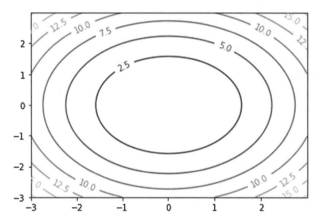

Figure 7-6. *Simple labeled contour*

You can also add a color bar to the output as follows:

```
out = plt.contour(X, Y, Z)
plt.clabel(out, inline=True,
           fontsize=10)
plt.colorbar(out)
plt.show()
```

Figure 7-7 shows the output.

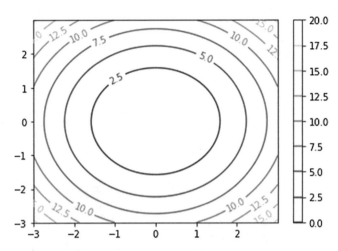

Figure 7-7. *Simple labeled contour with a color bar*

You can also set the colors of the contour as follows:

```
out = plt.contour(X, Y, Z,
                  colors='g')
plt.clabel(out, inline=True,
           fontsize=10)
plt.show()
```

Figure 7-8 shows the output.

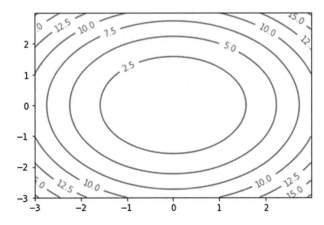

Figure 7-8. *Simple labeled contour with custom colors*

You can also have a filled contour. The styles are used to highlight the various areas in the contour visualization. Let's visualize filled contours as follows:

```
plt.contourf(X, Y, Z,
             hatches=['-', '/', '\\', '//'],
             cmap='cool',
             alpha=0.75)
plt.show()
```

Figure 7-9 shows the output.

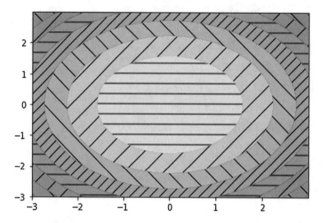

Figure 7-9. *Filled contour*

Visualizing Vectors with Stream Plots

Up to now, we have visualized scalar entities, which have magnitudes. All the visualizations you have learned about up to this point are great for scalars. Vectors, by contrast, are entities that have magnitude and direction. For example, force has a magnitude and a direction. A specific example is a magnetic force field. You can visualize vectors with stream plots. Let's create our own dataset to visualize this. We will create a mesh with X and Y. Then we will create U and V to show the magnitude.

```
Y, X = np.mgrid[-5:5:200j, -5:5:300j]
U = X**2 + Y**2
V = X + Y
```

You can create a simple stream plot as follows:

```
plt.streamplot(X, Y, U, V)
plt.show()
```

Figure 7-10 shows the output.

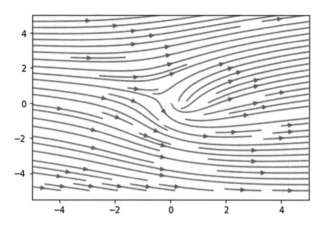

Figure 7-10. *Simple stream plot*

You can also have stream plots of variable densities as follows:

```
plt.streamplot(X, Y, U, V,
            density=[0.5, 0.75])
plt.show()
```

Figure 7-11 shows the output.

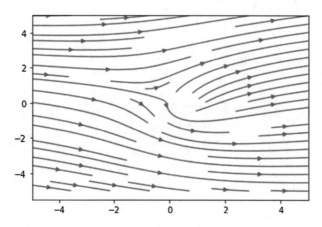

Figure 7-11. *Stream plot with variable densities*

You can also assign colors to the stream plot as follows:

```
plt.streamplot(X, Y, U, V, color=V,
          linewidth=1, cmap='cool')
plt.show()
```

Figure 7-12 shows the output.

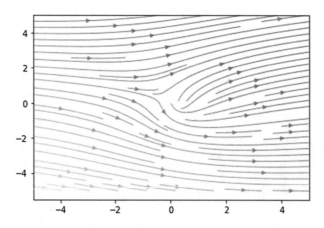

Figure 7-12. *Stream plot with variable colors*

You can also create a stream plot with variable line widths as follows:

```
plt.streamplot(X, Y, U, V,
               density=0.6,
               color='k',
               linewidth=X)
plt.show()
```

Figure 7-13 shows the output.

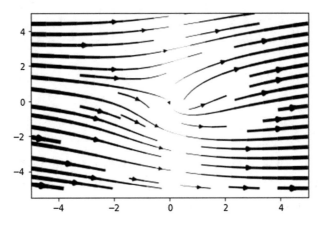

Figure 7-13. *Stream plot with variable line widths*

You can also use quiver plots for the vector visualizations as follows:

```
X = np.arange(-5, 5, 0.5)
Y = np.arange(-10, 10, 1)
U, V = np.meshgrid(X, Y)
plt.quiver(X, Y, U, V)
plt.show()
```

Figure 7-14 shows the output.

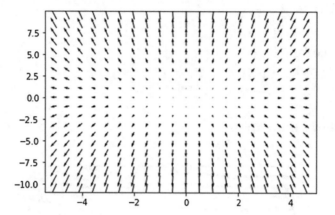

Figure 7-14. *Visualizing vector fields with a quiver plot*

Summary

In this chapter, you learned about histograms, contours, and stream plots.

In the next chapter, you will learn how to visualize images and audio. You will also learn interpolation methods for images.

CHAPTER 8

Image and Audio Visualization

In the previous chapter, you learned how to create visualizations with histograms, contours, and stream plots.

In this chapter, you will learn how to process and visualize images and audio with Matplotlib. Specifically, you will learn about the following topics in this chapter:

- Visualizing images

- Interpolation methods

- Audio visualization

- Audio processing

After reading this chapter, we will be able to visualize images and audio with Matplotlib.

Visualizing Images

You can read digital images with Matplotlib, which supports many image formats, although you do have to install a library called *pillow*. Install pillow as shown here:

```
!pip3 install pillow
```

I recommend that you create a fresh notebook for this chapter. Import the library with the following statements:

```
%matplotlib inline
import numpy as np
import matplotlib.pyplot as plt
```

© Ashwin Pajankar 2022
A. Pajankar, *Hands-on Matplotlib*, https://doi.org/10.1007/978-1-4842-7410-1_8

You can read digital images with the function imread() on Windows as follows:

```
img1 = plt.imread("D:/Dataset/4.2.03.tiff")
```

The code is similar for Linux and Mac, as follows:

```
img1 = plt.imread("~/Dataset/4.2.03.tiff")
```

Let's see the contents of the variable now, as shown here:

```
print(img1)
```

The output is as follows:

```
array([[[164, 150,  71],
        [ 63,  57,  31],
        [ 75,  43,  10],
        ...,
        [  5,   8,   5],
        [  2,   5,   0],
        [  4,   5,   2]]], dtype=uint8)
```

I have removed the middle part of the output to save space, but this is an Ndarray after all. We can confirm this with the following code:

```
type(img1)
```

The output is as follows:

```
numpy.ndarray
```

To learn more about the image, you can check the properties of the Ndarray that is storing the image data. A color image is stored as a 3D matrix, and each individual dimension of that matrix is used to visualize the intensity of the color channel. Color images are read and stored in red, green, blue (RGB) format. Since there are no colors in grayscale images, there is only a single plane (a 2D matrix) that stores the intensities of the grayscale values.

You can use the routine imshow() to show any Ndarray as an image as follows:

```
plt.imshow(img1)
plt.show()
```

Figure 8-1 shows the output.

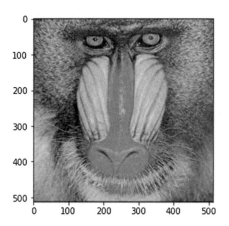

Figure 8-1. *Visualizing an image*

This is a color image. The Matplotlib library automatically detects that the image has multiple channels and shows it as a color image. However, it goofs up a little bit when we show grayscale images.

```
img2 = plt.imread("D:/Dataset/5.1.11.tiff")
plt.imshow(img2)
plt.show()
```

Figure 8-2 shows the output.

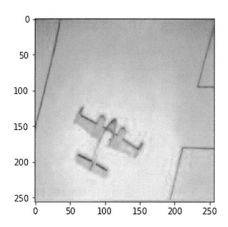

Figure 8-2. *Visualizing a grayscale image*

The image data is interpreted correctly, but there seems to be some problem with the color. For grayscale images, Matplotlib uses the default color map, so you have to manually specify the color map as follows:

```
plt.imshow(img2, cmap = 'gray')
plt.show()
```

Figure 8-3 shows the output.

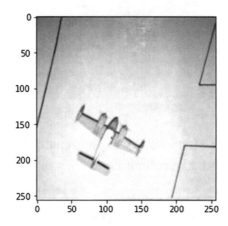

Figure 8-3. *Visualizing a grayscale image with the correct color map*

A color map is a matrix of values defining the colors for visualizations. Let's try another color map for the image, as shown here:

```
plt.imshow(img2, cmap = 'cool')
plt.show()
```

Figure 8-4 shows the output.

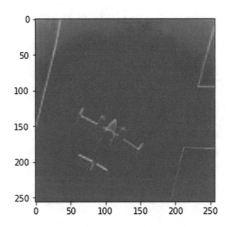

Figure 8-4. *Visualizing a grayscale image with a cool color map*

You can display a list of color maps in the current version of Matplotlib by using the following statement:

```
plt.colormaps()
```

The output is as follows:

```
['Accent',
 'Accent_r',
 .........
 'twilight_r',
 'twilight_shifted',
 'twilight_shifted_r',
 'viridis',
 'viridis_r',
 'winter',
 'winter_r']
```

I have removed a big portion of the output so that it will fit in the book. You can use any of these color maps for your visualization needs. As an exercise, try a few color maps with a grayscale image.

Image Masking

You can mask the areas of an image with a circle as follows:

```
import matplotlib.patches as patches
fig, ax = plt.subplots()
im = ax.imshow(img1)
patch = patches.Circle((245, 200),
                       radius=200,
                       transform=ax.transData)
im.set_clip_path(patch)

ax.axis('off')
plt.show()
```

In this code example, we are creating a circle with the routine Circle() at the XY co-ordinates 245, 200. The radius is 200 pixels. Also, we are clipping the image with the circle using the routine set_clip_path() and showing it. Figure 8-5 shows the output.

Figure 8-5. *Clipping an image with a circle*

Interpolation Methods

You can show a simple NumPy Ndarray as an image as follows:

```
img3 = [[1, 2, 3, 4],
        [5, 6, 7, 8],
        [9, 10, 11, 12],
```

```
        [13, 14, 15, 16]]
plt.imshow(img3)
plt.show()
```

Figure 8-6 shows the output.

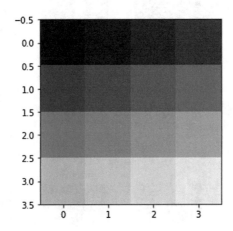

Figure 8-6. *NumPy Ndarray as an image*

The image is using no interpolation method for visualization. We can demo interpolation methods as follows:

```
methods = ['none', 'antialiased', 'nearest', 'bilinear',
           'bicubic', 'spline16', 'spline36', 'hanning',
           'hamming', 'hermite', 'kaiser', 'quadric',
           'catrom', 'gaussian', 'bessel', 'mitchell',
           'sinc', 'lanczos', 'blackman']

fig, axs = plt.subplots(nrows=4, ncols=6, figsize=(9, 6),
                        subplot_kw={'xticks': [], 'yticks': []})

for ax, interp_method in zip(axs.flat, methods):
    ax.imshow(img3, interpolation=interp_method, cmap='hot')
    ax.set_title(str(interp_method))

plt.tight_layout()
plt.show()
```

In this code example, we are simply showing the same Ndarray with all the interpolation methods available in Matplotlib. Figure 8-7 shows the output.

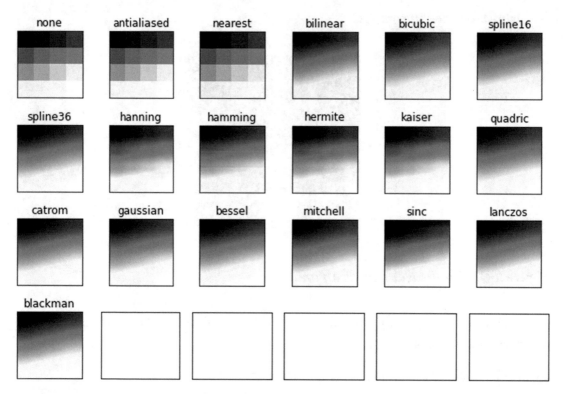

Figure 8-7. *Demo of interpolation methods*

Audio Visualization

You can use Matplotlib to visualize audio. You just need the SciPy library to read an audio file and store that data to an Ndarray. Let's install it, as shown here:

```
!pip3 install scipy
```

Let's import all the required libraries, as shown here:

```
%matplotlib inline
import matplotlib.pyplot as plt
from scipy.io import wavfile
```

Let's read an audio file now. I am reading a WAV file as follows:

```
samplerate, data = wavfile.read('sample.wav')
```

Let's see the sampling rate of the music, as shown here:

```
print(samplerate)
```

The output is as follows:

```
44100
```

This (44.1 kHz) is a common sampling rate. You can read an informative article about audio sampling rates at https://www.izotope.com/en/learn/digital-audio-basics-sample-rate-and-bit-depth.html.

You can also display the data as follows:

```
print(data)
```

The data is as follows:

```
[[-204    23]
 [-233    32]
 [-191    34]
 ...
 [ 646   676]
 [ 679   707]
 [ 623   650]]
```

You can check the properties of the audio as follows:

```
print(type(data))
print(data.shape)
print(data.ndim)
print(data.dtype)
print(data.size)
print(data.nbytes)
```

The output is as follows:

```
<class 'numpy.ndarray'>
(2601617, 2)
2
int16
5203234
10406468
```

The audio data is retrieved and stored in the NumPy, as you have seen. It is stored in a 2D matrix. Suppose that there are N data points (also known as *sample points*) for the audio data; then the size of the NumPy array is N×2. As you can see, the audio has two channels, left and right. So, each channel in stored in a separate array of size N, and thus we have N×2. This is known as *stereo audio*. In this example, we have 2,601,617 points (samples). Each point or sample is represented using a pair of integers of 16 bits (2 bytes). Thus, each sample needs four bytes. So, we can compute the total raw memory required for storing the audio data by multiplying the sample size by 4. When we visualize audio, we show the value of both channels of the sample. Let's visualize the first 2,000 data points as follows:

```
plt.plot(data[:2000])
plt.show()
```

Figure 8-8 shows the output.

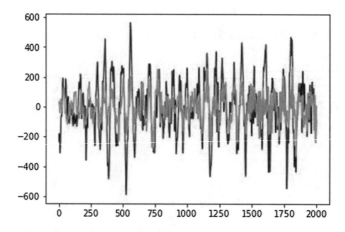

Figure 8-8. *Visualization of an audio file*

You can check the number of audio samples as follows:

```
samples = data.shape[0]
print(samples)
```

The output is as follows:

```
2601617
```

You can create a different visualization of the data as follows:

```
plt.plot(data[:10*samplerate])
plt.show()
```

Figure 8-9 shows the output.

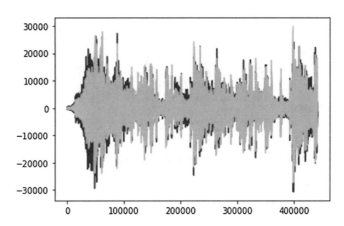

Figure 8-9. *Visualization of an audio file*

Let's separate the data for both channels as follows:

```
channel1 = data[:, 0]
channel2 = data[:, 1]
print(channel1, channel2)
```

The output is as follows:

```
[-204 -233 -191 ...  646  679  623] [ 23  32  34 ... 676 707 650]
```

Let's visualize the data as follows:

```
plt.subplot(2, 1, 1)
plt.plot(channel1[:10*samplerate])
plt.subplot(2, 1, 2)
plt.plot(channel2[:10*samplerate], c='g')
plt.show()
```

Figure 8-10 shows the output.

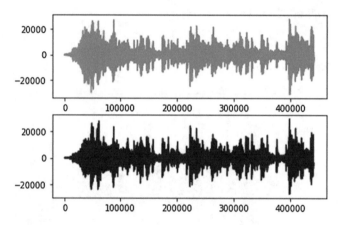

Figure 8-10. *Visualization of both audio channels*

Audio Processing

The Fourier transform converts the data represented as waves in the time domain into the frequency domain. So, when you compute the Fourier transform and visualize it, you are seeing the representation in the frequency domain.

The fast Fourier transform (FFT) is an efficient method of computing a Fourier transform of the waveform data. FFT reduces the number of computations, which is why it is speedy; that's why it is known as a *fast* Fourier transform. Let's compute the fast Fourier transform of the audio signal as follows:

```
import scipy.fftpack
datafft = scipy.fftpack.fft(data)
fftabs = abs(datafft)
print(fftabs)
```

The output is as follows:

```
[[ 181.   227.]
 [ 201.   265.]
 [ 157.   225.]
 ...
 [1322.    30.]
 [1386.    28.]
 [1273.    27.]]
```

Let's compute the frequency and plot the graph as follows:

```
freqs = scipy.fftpack.fftfreq( samples, 1/samplerate )
plt.plot(freqs, fftabs)
plt.show()
```

Figure 8-11 shows the output.

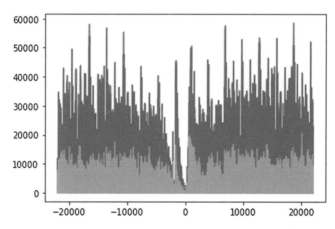

Figure 8-11. *Visualization of FFT*

Summary

In this chapter, you learned how to create visualizations for images and audio.

In the next chapter, you will learn how to visualize pie and polar charts.

CHAPTER 9

Pie and Polar Charts

In the previous chapter, you learned how to visualize and process images and audio with Matplotlib and SciPy.

In this chapter, you will learn how to create pie and polar charts with Matplotlib.

Pie Charts

Let's learn the basics of the pie charts first. As the name indicates, a pie chart is a circle that is divided radially depending on the data. Imagine an apple pie or a pizza cut into slices. A pie chart fits that description well; however, unlike pizza or pies, which are usually divided symmetrically, a pie chart is not necessarily radially symmetrical. It all depends on the data to be visualized.

Let's get started. I recommend creating a new notebook for this exercise.

```
%matplotlib inline
import matplotlib.pyplot as plt
import numpy as np
```

Let's create the data to be visualized, as follows:

```
data = np.array([35, 25, 25, 15])
```

Let's visualize the data with a simple pie chart as follows:

```
plt.pie(data)
plt.show()
```

© Ashwin Pajankar 2022
A. Pajankar, *Hands-on Matplotlib*, https://doi.org/10.1007/978-1-4842-7410-1_9

Figure 9-1 shows the output.

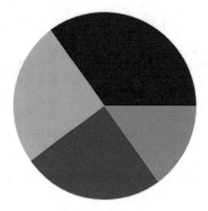

Figure 9-1. *A simple pie chart*

Let's add labels as follows:

```
mylabels = ['A', 'B', 'C', 'D']
plt.pie(data,
        labels = mylabels)
plt.show()
```

Figure 9-2 shows the output.

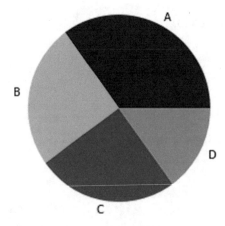

Figure 9-2. *A simple pie chart with labels*

You can even separate the parts of the pie a bit, as follows:

```
explode = [0.0, 0.05, 0.1, 0.15]
plt.pie(data,
        labels = mylabels,
        explode = explode)
plt.show()
```

The output will have the parts of the pie separated as per the values in the explode argument. Figure 9-3 shows the output.

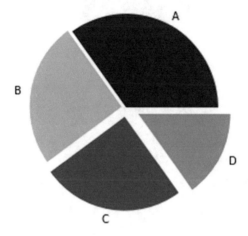

Figure 9-3. *A simple pie chart with labels and explosion*

You can also enable shadows as follows:

```
plt.pie(data,
        labels = mylabels,
        explode = explode,
        shadow = True)
plt.show()
```

Figure 9-4 shows the output.

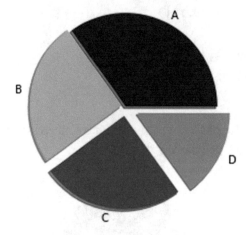

Figure 9-4. *A simple pie chart with shadows*

You can also add a legend to the output as follows:

```
plt.pie(data,
        labels = mylabels,
        explode = explode,
        shadow = True)
plt.legend()
plt.show()
```

Figure 9-5 shows the output.

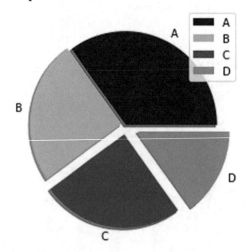

Figure 9-5. *A simple pie chart with a legend*

You can add a title for the legend as follows:

```
plt.pie(data,
        labels = mylabels,
        explode = explode,
        shadow = True)
plt.legend(title='Data :')
plt.show()
```

Figure 9-6 shows the output.

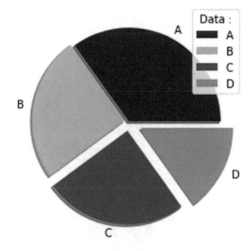

Figure 9-6. *A simple pie chart with legends and a title for the legend*

You've just learned how to create polar graphs.

Polar Charts

You can also create polar graphs that are in the shape of pie charts. However, a fundamental difference from the Cartesian (X-Y) coordinate system is that in a polar chart the coordinate system is radially arranged, so you need the angle (theta) and distance from the origin (*r* is the radius) to visualize a point or set of points. Let's create a dataset as follows:

```
N = 20
theta = np.linspace(0.0, 2 * np.pi, N)
r = 10 * np.random.rand(N)
```

The set of points can be visualized as follows:

```
plt.subplot(projection='polar')
plt.bar(theta, r, bottom=0.0,
        color=['r', 'g', 'b'], alpha=0.2)
plt.show()
```

Figure 9-7 shows the output.

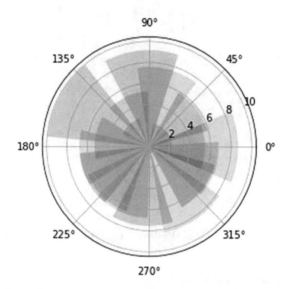

Figure 9-7. *A simple polar graph*

You can see that this creates a bar visualization, as shown in Figure 9-7. There are a few useful video tutorials on YouTube where you can learn more about creating visualizations in the polar coordinate system.

```
https://www.youtube.com/watch?v=mDT_DG_AOJA
https://www.youtube.com/watch?v=GMcRqtm4mNo
https://www.youtube.com/watch?v=VmQ1isayjJI
```

Let's create a simple graph. Let's create the dataset for it as shown here:

```
r = np.arange(0, 5, 0.2)
theta = 2 * np.pi * r
plt.subplot(projection='polar')
plt.plot(theta, r)
plt.show()
```

This creates a simple linear visualization on a polar graph. As this is a polar graph, you will see a spiral-like structure, as shown in Figure 9-8.

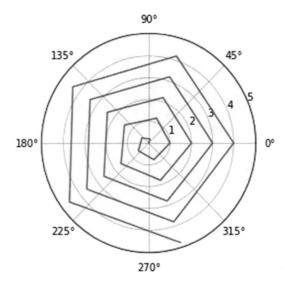

Figure 9-8. *A simple linear visualization on a polar graph*

This is not a perfect spiral as the distance between the consecutive points is 0.2. If you reduce the distance, then you will get a perfect spiral. Let's tweak the data as follows:

```
r = np.arange(0, 5, 0.01)
theta = 2 * np.pi * r
plt.subplot(projection='polar')
plt.plot(theta, r)
plt.show()
```

This creates a perfect spiral, as shown in Figure 9-9.

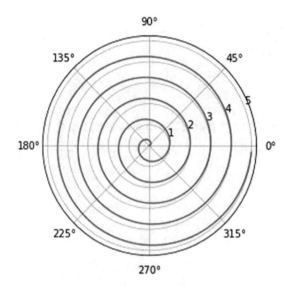

Figure 9-9. *A spiral visualization*

Let's see a couple of examples of scatter plots on a polar graph. To start, prepare the data as shown here:

```
N = 150
r = np.random.rand(N)
theta = 2 * np.pi * np.random.rand(N)
size = r * 100
```

You can visualize this as follows:

```
plt.subplot(projection='polar')
plt.scatter(theta, r, c=theta,
            s=size, cmap='hsv',
            alpha=0.5)
plt.show()
```

Figure 9-10 shows the output.

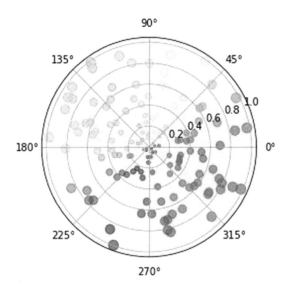

Figure 9-10. *A scatter plot*

You can also show part of the visualization by setting the start and end angles, as follows:

```
fig = plt.figure()
ax = fig.add_subplot(projection='polar')
c = ax.scatter(theta, r, c=theta,
               s=size, cmap='hsv',
               alpha=0.5)
ax.set_thetamin(0)
ax.set_thetamax(90)
plt.show()
```

The output shows only part of the entire polar graph, as shown in Figure 9-11.

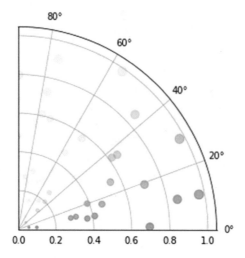

Figure 9-11. *A partial scatter plot*

As an exercise, you may want to create partial spirals and bar graphs.

Summary

In this chapter, learned how to create pie charts and polar charts in detail.

In the next chapter, you will learn how to create a few more visualizations, namely, using the routines pColor(), pColormesh(), and colorbar().

CHAPTER 10

Working with Colors

In the previous chapter, you learned how to visualize pie charts and polar charts with Matplotlib.

In this chapter, you will learn how to work with colors. The following are the routines you will learn to use in this chapter:

- pcolor()
- pcolormesh()
- colorbar()

After reading this chapter, we will be able to work with colors in Matplotlib.

pcolor()

The routine pcolor() creates a pseudocolor plot with a rectangular (nonsquare) grid. Pseudocolor means the object or image is rendered in colors different than those in which it was recorded. Let's create a new notebook for this chapter, as shown here:

```
%matplotlib inline
import matplotlib.pyplot as plt
import numpy as np
```

Let's create a nonsquare matrix and use the routine pcolor() to visualize it, as shown here:

```
data = np.random.rand(5, 6)
plt.pcolor(data)
plt.show()
```

© Ashwin Pajankar 2022
A. Pajankar, *Hands-on Matplotlib*, https://doi.org/10.1007/978-1-4842-7410-1_10

Figure 10-1 shows the output.

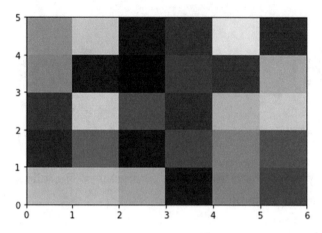

Figure 10-1. *A simple demonstration of pcolor()*

You can also use custom color maps as follows:

```
plt.pcolor(data, cmap='YlGnBu_r')
plt.show()
```

Figure 10-2 shows the output.

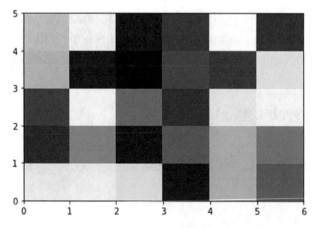

Figure 10-2. *A simple demonstration of pcolor() with color maps*

Let's now try adding shading. Let's create a new dataset, as follows:

```
N = 100
X, Y = np.meshgrid(np.linspace(-5, 5, N),
                   np.linspace(-4, 4, N))
Z = (X**2 + Y**2)
```

You can visualize it as follows:

```
plt.pcolor(X, Y, Z,
           cmap='YlGnBu_r',
           shading='auto')
plt.show()
```

Figure 10-3 shows the output.

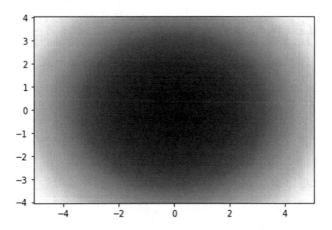

Figure 10-3. *Shading*

You can also create a visualization with nearest as the method for shading. In this shading technique, each grid point has a color centered on it and it extends halfway between the adjacent grid centers.In this shading technique, each grid point has a color centered on it and it extends halfway between the adjacent grid centers. The example is as follows:

```
plt.pcolor(X, Y, Z,
           cmap='YlGnBu_r',
           shading='nearest')
plt.show()
```

Figure 10-4 shows the output.

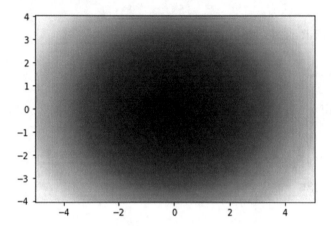

Figure 10-4. *Shading with nearest*

pcolormesh()

The routine polormesh() behaves in the same way as pcolor(); however, it renders large datasets much faster. Let's create a visualization of the same dataset used for Figure 10-4 but with polormesh(). The code is as follows:

```
plt.pcolormesh(X, Y, Z,
            cmap='YlGnBu_r',
            shading='auto')
plt.show()
```

Let's see an example with shading and a color map, as shown here:

```
nrows = ncols = 5
x = np.arange(ncols + 1)
y = np.arange(nrows + 1)
z = np.arange(nrows * ncols).reshape(nrows, ncols)
plt.pcolormesh(x, y, z,
            shading='flat',
            cmap='coolwarm')
plt.show()
```

Figure 10-5 shows the output.

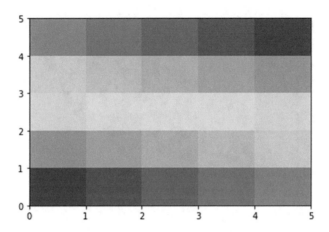

Figure 10-5. *Using pcolormesh() with shading and a color map*

Run the following example with different arguments:

```
plt.pcolormesh(x, y, z,
               shading='auto',
               cmap='cool')
plt.show()
```

You can also apply a simple geometric transformation to the dataset as follows:

```
z = np.random.rand(6, 10)
x = np.arange(0, 10, 1)
y = np.arange(4, 10, 1)
T = 0.5
X, Y = np.meshgrid(x, y)
X = X + T * Y
Y = Y + T * X
plt.pcolormesh(X, Y, Z,
               shading='auto')
plt.show()
```

Figure 10-6 shows the output.

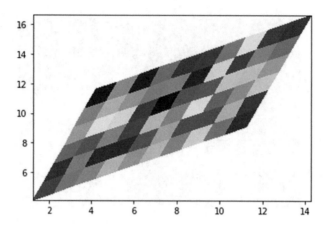

Figure 10-6. *Using polormesh() with a simple transformation*

colorbar()

You can also add a color bar that corelates with the magnitude of data points in the visualization. The routine colorbar() does the trick. The following is the code:

```
N = 100
X, Y = np.meshgrid(np.linspace(-5, 5, N),
                   np.linspace(-5, 5, N))
Z = (X**2 + Y**2)
img = plt.imshow(Z, cmap='YlGnBu_r')
plt.colorbar(img)
plt.show()
```

Figure 10-7 shows the output.

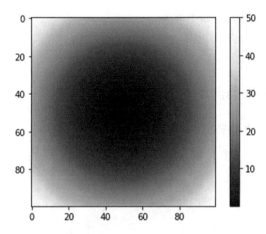

Figure 10-7. *Simple color bar*

You can shrink the color bar and change its position as follows:

```
img = plt.imshow(Z, cmap='coolwarm')
plt.colorbar(img, location='left', shrink=0.6)
plt.show()
```

Figure 10-8 shows the output.

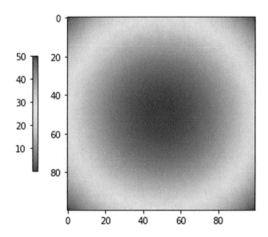

Figure 10-8. *Shrunken color bar*

You can also extend the color bar as follows:

```
img = plt.imshow(Z, cmap='coolwarm')
plt.colorbar(img, extend='both')
plt.show()
```

Figure 10-9 shows the output.

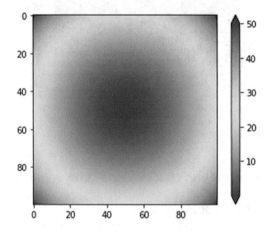

Figure 10-9. *Extended color bar*

Summary

In this chapter, you learned how to work with colors. In the next chapter, you will learn how to create 3D visualizations.

CHAPTER 11

3D Visualizations in Matplotlib

In the previous chapter, you learned how to work with colors in Matplotlib.

In this chapter, you will learn how to work with 3D visualizations. The following are the topics you will learn about in this chapter:

- Plotting 3D lines, scatter plots, and contours

- Working with wireframes, surfaces, and sample data

- Plotting bar graphs

- Plotting quiver and stem plots

- Working with 3D volumes

Wireframes, surfaces, and 3D contours are used to show volumetric data. Bar graphs are used to show categorical data. Quiver plots are used for visualizing vectors. After reading this chapter, you will be able to work with all these 3D visualizations in Matplotlib.

Getting Ready

I recommend that you create a new notebook for all the examples in this chapter. To get ready, you need to install one additional library as follows:

```
!pip3 install PyQt5
```

Qt is a cross-platform library for GUI. PyQt5 is the Python binding for Qt. Once the library is installed, you can use the following magical command to force Jupyter Notebook to show the visualizations in a separate QT window:

```
%matplotlib qt
```

© Ashwin Pajankar 2022
A. Pajankar, *Hands-on Matplotlib*, https://doi.org/10.1007/978-1-4842-7410-1_11

So, when you create visualizations, you are also able to interact with them. Let's learn the basics. First, we import all the required libraries, as shown here:

```
import numpy as np
import matplotlib.pyplot as plt
from mpl_toolkits import mplot3d
```

Then we create a figure object, as shown here:

```
fig = plt.figure()
```

Then we create a 3D axis as follows:

```
ax = plt.axes(projection='3d')
```

You have to add the code for the visualization after this. However, for this example, you will create the visualization for an empty figure and axes with the following line:

```
plt.show()
```

Figure 11-1 shows the output.

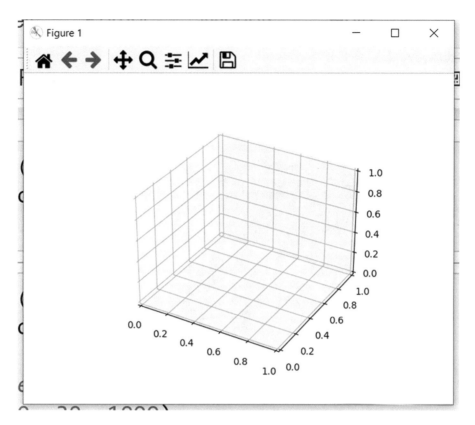

Figure 11-1. *An empty and interactive 3D visualization*

You can interact with this visualization and change the orientation of it by using your mouse. Take the time to explore all the interactive possibilities before proceeding.

Plotting 3D Lines

Let's plot a 3D line. Let's create a figure and axes, as shown here:

```
fig = plt.figure()
ax = plt.axes(projection='3d')
```

Let's create 3D data as follows:

```
z = np.linspace(0, 30, 1000)
x = np.sin(z)
y = np.cos(z)
```

You can create a 3D plot as follows:

```
ax.plot3D(x, y, z, 'red')
plt.show()
```

Figure 11-2 shows the output.

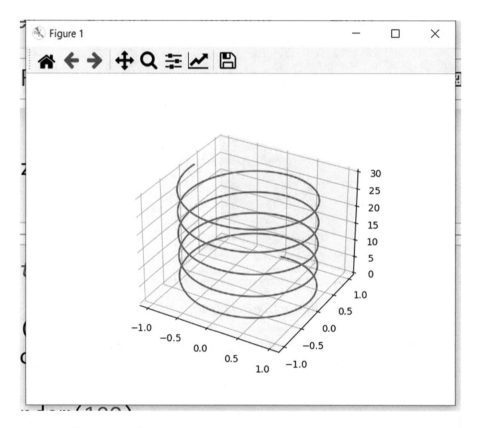

Figure 11-2. *3D linear plot*

3D Scatter Plots

You can create random points and show them with a 3D scatter as follows. Let's create a figure and axes first, as shown here:

```
fig = plt.figure()
ax = plt.axes(projection='3d')
```

You can create the random data points as follows:

```
y = np.random.random(100)
x = np.random.random(100)
z = np.random.random(100)
```

The points can be visualized with a scatter plot as follows:

```
ax.scatter3D(x, y, z,  cmap='cool');
plt.show()
```

Figure 11-3 shows the output.

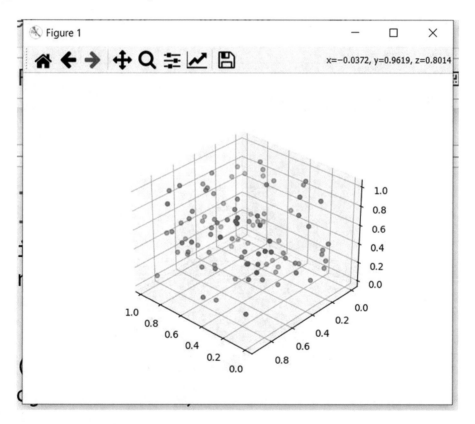

Figure 11-3. *3D scatter plot*

3D Contours

You can create 3D contours with the functions contour() and contour3D(). Let's create some data to be visualized.

```
x = np.linspace(-10, 10, 30)
y = np.linspace(-10, 10, 30)
X, Y = np.meshgrid(x, y)
Z = np.sin(np.sqrt(X ** 2 + Y ** 2))
```

You can create a contour as follows:

```
fig = plt.figure()
ax = fig.add_subplot(projection='3d')
ax.contour(X, Y, Z, 50, cmap='coolwarm')
plt.show()
```

Figure 11-4 shows the output.

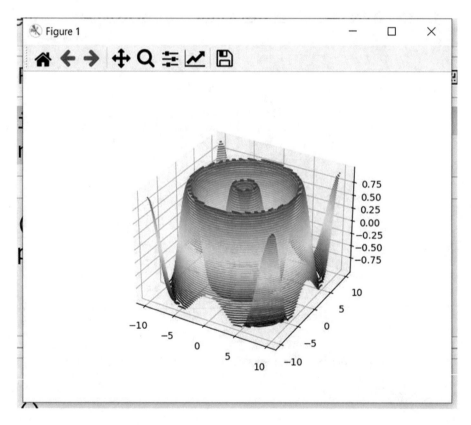

Figure 11-4. *3D contour plot*

You can obtain similar output as visualized in Figure 11-4 using the following code:

```
fig = plt.figure()
ax = plt.axes(projection='3d')
ax.contour3D(X, Y, Z, 40,
             cmap='coolwarm')
plt.show()
```

You can also create a filled contour with the function contourf() as follows:

```
fig = plt.figure()
ax = fig.add_subplot(projection='3d')
ax.contourf(X, Y, Z, 50, cmap='coolwarm')
plt.show()
```

Wireframes, Surfaces, and Sample Data

You can plot a wireframe of the same dataset as follows:

```
fig = plt.figure()
ax = plt.axes(projection='3d')
ax.plot_wireframe(X, Y, Z, color='Green')
ax.set_title('wireframe')
plt.show()
```

Figure 11-5 shows the output.

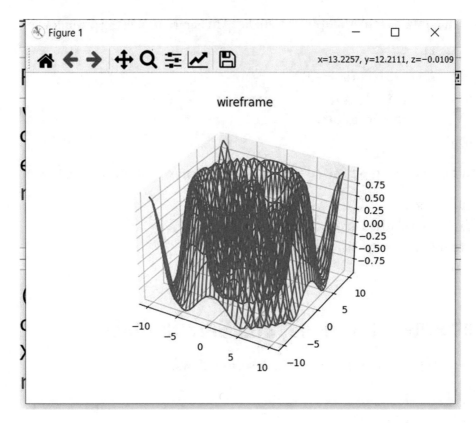

Figure 11-5. *3D wireframe*

The same data can be visualized as a 3D surface as follows:

```
fig = plt.figure()
ax = plt.axes(projection='3d')
ax.plot_surface(X, Y, Z, color='Blue')
ax.set_title('Surface Plot')
plt.show()
```

Figure 11-6 shows the output.

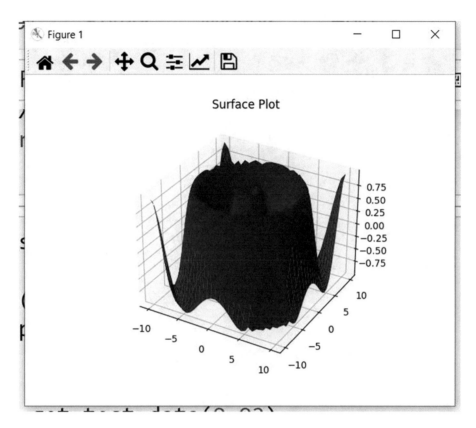

Figure 11-6. *3D surface*

You can also use the sample data that comes with the Matplotlib library for demonstrating visualizations. The function get_test_data() can fetch that sample data as follows:

```
from mpl_toolkits.mplot3d import axes3d
fig = plt.figure()
ax = fig.add_subplot(projection='3d')
X, Y, Z = axes3d.get_test_data(0.02)
ax.plot_wireframe(X, Y, Z,
                rstride=10,
                cstride=10)
plt.show()
```

Figure 11-7 shows the output.

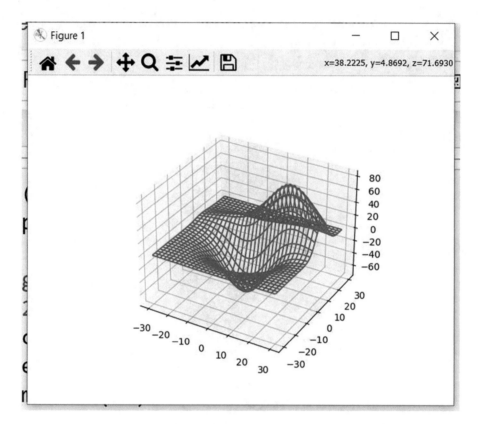

Figure 11-7. *Visualizing the test data*

As an exercise, try to create a surface and contour with the test data.

Bar Graphs

You can show 2D bars in 3D axes. Let's create a figure and axes, as shown here:

```
fig = plt.figure()
ax = fig.add_subplot(projection='3d')
```

Let's define colors for the bars.

```
colors = ['r', 'g', 'b', 'c', 'm', 'y','k']
yticks = [0, 1, 2, 3, 4, 5, 6]
```

Now, let's create bar graphs with the defined colors with the following loop:

```
for c, k in zip(colors, yticks):
    x = np.arange(25)
    y = np.random.rand(25)
    ax.bar(x, y, zs=k, zdir='y',
           color=c, alpha=0.8)
plt.show()
```

Figure 11-8 shows the output.

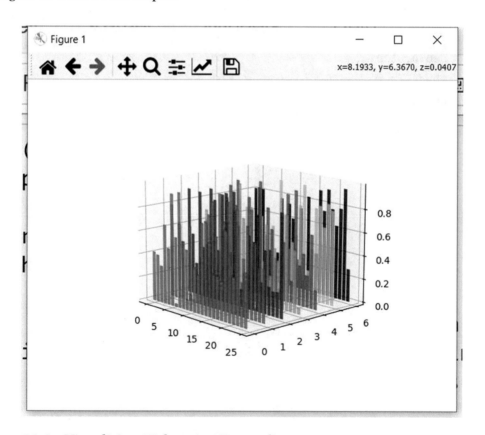

Figure 11-8. *Visualizing 2D bars in 3D coordinates*

You can also create a 3D bar graph with Matplotlib. Let's create the data first, as shown here:

```
fig = plt.figure()
ax = fig.add_subplot(projection='3d')

x = np.arange(10) * np.arange(10)
y = np.arange(10) * np.arange(10)
x, y = np.meshgrid(x, y)
x, y = x.ravel(), y.ravel()
top = x + y
bottom = np.zeros_like(top)
width = depth = 5
```

You can then show this as 3D bars as follows:

```
ax.bar3d(x, y, bottom, width,
         depth, top,
         shade=True,
         color='g')
plt.show()
```

Figure 11-9 shows the output.

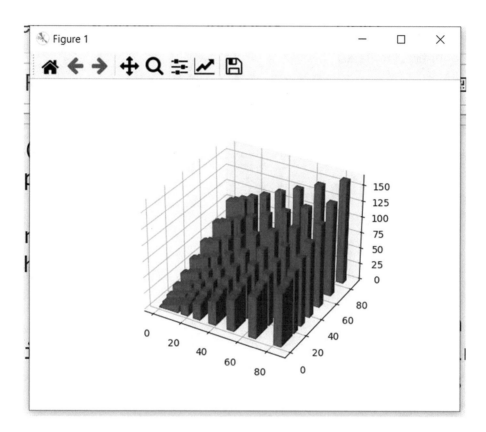

Figure 11-9. *Visualizing 3D bars*

Quiver and Stem Plots

A quiver plot is used to represent directional entities (for example, vectors). Let's define the data, as shown here:

```
fig = plt.figure()
ax = fig.add_subplot(projection='3d')
x = y = z = np.arange(-0.1, 1, 0.2)
X, Y, Z = np.meshgrid(x, y, z)
u = np.cos(np.pi * X) * np.sin(np.pi * Y) * np.sin(np.pi * Z)
v = -np.sin(np.pi * X) * np.cos(np.pi * Y) * np.sin(np.pi * Z)
w = np.sin(np.pi * X) * np.sin(np.pi * Y) * np.cos(np.pi * Z)
```

Finally, you can visualize the data as follows:

```
ax.quiver(X, Y, Z, u, v, w,
          length=0.1,
          normalize=True)
plt.show()
```

Figure 11-10 shows the output.

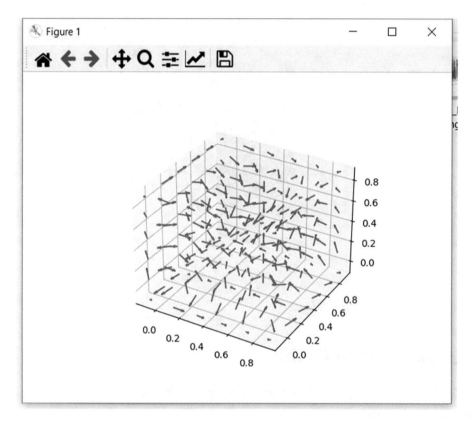

Figure 11-10. *Quiver plots*

You can also create stem plots where perpendicular lines are drawn in the visualization. Let's use trigonometric functions to define the data, as shown here:

```
fig = plt.figure()
ax = fig.add_subplot(projection='3d')
theta = np.linspace(0, 2 * np.pi)
```

```
x = np.sin(theta)
y = np.cos(theta)
z = np.cos(theta)
```

You can visualize the stem plot as follows:

```
ax.stem(x, y, z)
plt.show()
```

Figure 11-11 shows the output.

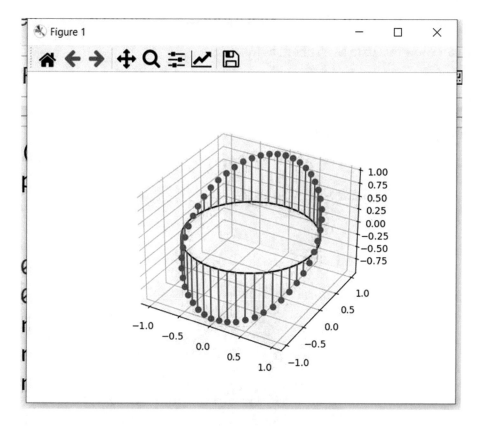

Figure 11-11. *Stem plot*

3D Volumes

You can show 3D volumetric data as enclosed surfaces. Let's create such data as follows:

```
fig = plt.figure()
ax = fig.add_subplot(projection='3d')
u = np.linspace(0, 2 * np.pi, 100)
v = np.linspace(0, np.pi, 100)
x = 10 * np.outer(np.cos(u), np.sin(v))
y = 10 * np.outer(np.sin(u), np.sin(v))
z = 10 * np.outer(np.ones(np.size(u)), np.cos(v))
```

You can show this data as a sphere as follows:

```
ax.plot_surface(x, y, z)
plt.show()
```

Figure 11-12 shows the output.

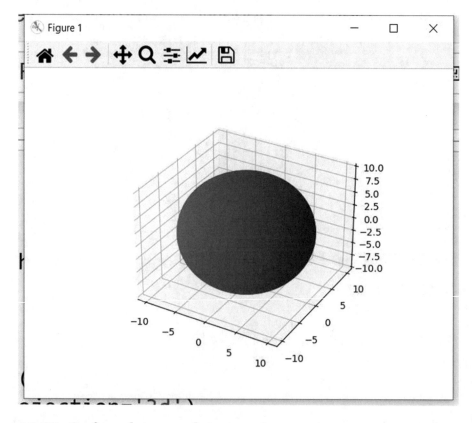

Figure 11-12. *Surface plot as a volume*

You can also use the function voxels() to visualize a volume as follows:

```
ma = np.random.randint(1, 3, size=(3, 3, 3))
fig = plt.figure()
ax = plt.axes(projection='3d')
ax.voxels(ma, edgecolor='k')
plt.show()
```

Figure 11-13 shows the output.

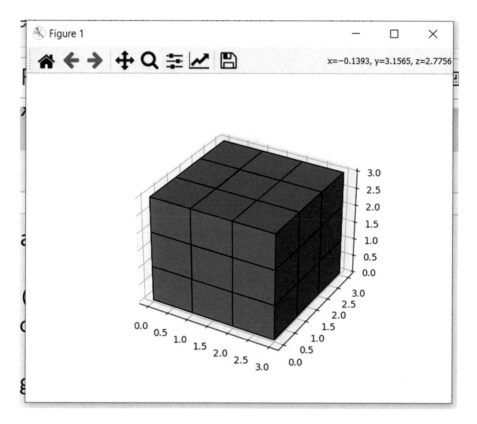

Figure 11-13. *3D volume plot*

Summary

In this chapter, you learned how to work with 3D visualizations. Wireframes, surfaces, and 3D contours are used to show volumetric data. Bar graphs are used to show categorical data. Quiver plots are used for visualizing vectors.

In the next chapter, you will learn how to create animations.

CHAPTER 12

Animations with Matplotlib

In the previous chapter, you learned how to work with 3D visualizations in Matplotlib.

In this chapter, you will learn how to work with animations. The following are the topics you will learn in this chapter:

- Animation basics
- Celluloid library

After reading this chapter, you will be able to work with animations in Matplotlib and another useful library.

Animation Basics

In this section, you will learn how to create animations with Matplotlib. First let's create a new notebook for this chapter. Then import the following libraries:

```
%matplotlib qt
import numpy as np
from matplotlib import pyplot as plt
from matplotlib.animation import FuncAnimation
```

Let's define the objects, in other words, the figure, axes, and plot, as follows:

```
fig = plt.figure()
ax = plt.axes(xlim=(0, 4), ylim=(-2, 2))
line, = ax.plot([], [], lw=3)
```

© Ashwin Pajankar 2022
A. Pajankar, *Hands-on Matplotlib*, https://doi.org/10.1007/978-1-4842-7410-1_12

Let's define the function init(), which will initialize the animation and set the data for the animation, as shown here:

```
def init():
    line.set_data([], [])
    return line,
```

Let's define an animation function, as shown here:

```
def animate(i):
    x = np.linspace(0, 4, 1000)
    y = np.sin(2 * np.pi * (x - 0.01 * i))
    line.set_data(x, y)
    return line,
```

This function accepts the frame number as an argument (in this case the variable named i) and renders the frame for animation.

Now that we have defined the components, let's create an animation object using the function call FuncAnimation(). It accepts the created functions as arguments. It also accepts the number of frames and the interval as arguments. The argument for the parameter blit is True. This means that only the parts of the plot that have changed are redrawn.

```
anim = FuncAnimation(fig, animate,
                     init_func=init,
                     frames=1000,
                     interval=10,
                     blit=True)
```

You can also save the animation as a GIF as follows:

```
anim.save('sine_wave.gif', writer='pillow')
```

Figure 12-1 shows the output.

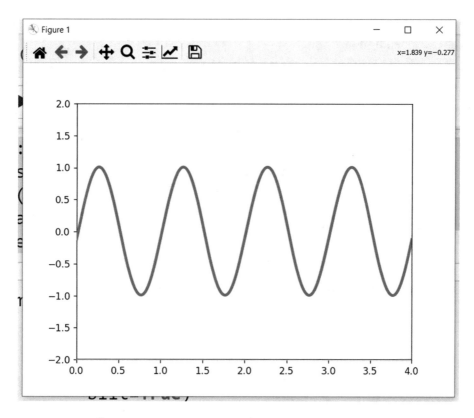

Figure 12-1. *Visualizing a sine wave*

You can interact with animation and change the orientation with your mouse. Explore all the interactive possibilities before proceeding further.

You can create a progressive spiral, as shown here:

```
fig = plt.figure()
ax = plt.axes(xlim=(-50, 50), ylim=(-50, 50))
line, = ax.plot([], [], lw=2)
def init():
    line.set_data([], [])
    return line,
xdata, ydata = [], []
def animate(i):
    t = 0.2*i
```

```
    x = t*np.cos(t)
    y = t*np.sin(t)
    xdata.append(x)
    ydata.append(y)
    line.set_data(xdata, ydata)
    return line,
anim = FuncAnimation(fig, animate,
                          init_func=init,
                          frames=3000,
                          interval=5,
                          blit=True)
```

Figure 12-2 shows the output.

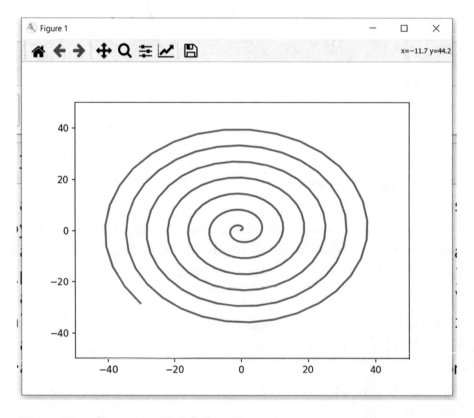

Figure 12-2. *Visualizing a spiral animation*

Celluloid Library

You can use another simple library called Celluloid for animation. Let's install it as follows:

```
!pip3 install celluloid
```

You can import it as follows:

```
from celluloid import Camera
```

Let's create a figure and camera object as follows:

```
fig = plt.figure()
camera = Camera(fig)
```

Let's create the frames of an animation and save them in memory with the function called camera.snap(), as follows:

```
for i in range(10):
    plt.plot([i] * 10)
    camera.snap()
```

Let's create the animation as follows:

```
animation = camera.animate()
```

Figure 12-3 shows the output.

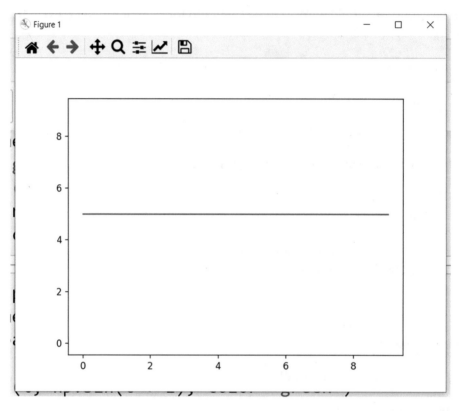

Figure 12-3. *Animation with the Celluloid library*

You can also create a sine wave as follows:

```
fig, axes = plt.subplots()
camera = Camera(fig)
t = np.linspace(0, 2 * np.pi, 128, endpoint=False)
for i in t:
    plt.plot(t, np.sin(t + i), color='green')
    camera.snap()
animation = camera.animate()
```

Figure 12-4 shows the output.

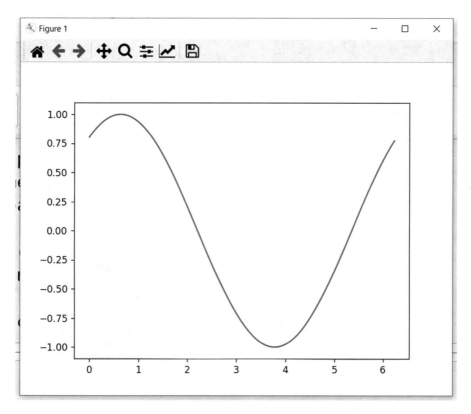

Figure 12-4. *Sine wave animation with the Celluloid library*

Another example with a bar graph is as follows:

```
fig, axes = plt.subplots()
camera = Camera(fig)
y = np.arange(5)
for i in y:
    plt.bar( np.random.rand(5)*10 , y)
    camera.snap()
animation = camera.animate()
```

Figure 12-5 shows the output.

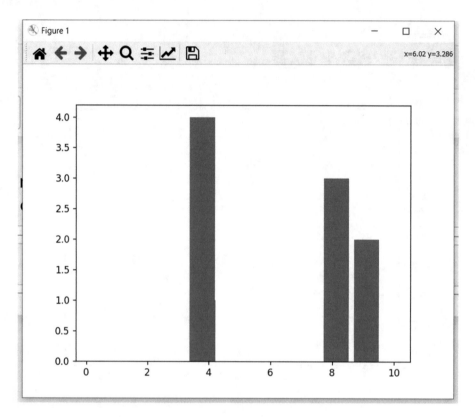

Figure 12-5. *Bar graph animation with the Celluloid library*

Summary

In this chapter, you learned how to work with animations.

In the next chapter, you will learn how to do even more with Matplotlib.

CHAPTER 13

More Visualizations with Matplotlib

In the previous chapter, you learned how to work with animations in Matplotlib.

In this chapter, you will learn a few more techniques for using Matplotlib. This chapter is the culmination of all the knowledge you have gained up to now. The chapter has an assortment of techniques for using Matplotlib that I did not cover in the earlier chapters. Specifically, the following are the topics you will learn in this chapter:

- Visualizing a function as an image and a contour

- Using 3D vignettes

- Decorating scatter plots

- Working with time plots and signals

- Working with filled plots, step plots, and hexbins

- Using XKCD style

After reading this chapter, you will be able to create all sorts of new visualizations in Matplotlib.

Visualizing a Function as an Image and a Contour

Let's visualize a numerical function. Import all the needed libraries as follows:

```
%matplotlib inline
import numpy as np
import matplotlib.pyplot as plt
```

© Ashwin Pajankar 2022
A. Pajankar, *Hands-on Matplotlib*, https://doi.org/10.1007/978-1-4842-7410-1_13

Let's define the function as follows:

```
def f(x, y):
    return (x ** 3 + y ** 2)
```

Let's visualize it as an image, as follows:

```
n = 10
x = np.linspace(-3, 3, 8 * n)
y = np.linspace(-3, 3, 6 * n)
X, Y = np.meshgrid(x, y)
Z = f( X, Y )
plt.imshow(Z, interpolation='nearest',
            cmap = 'cool', origin='lower')
plt.axis('off')
plt.show()
```

Figure 13-1 shows the output.

Figure 13-1. *Visualizing a function as an image*

You can visualize the function as a contour too.

```
n = 256
x = np.linspace(-3, 3, n)
y = np.linspace(-3, 3, n)
X, Y = np.meshgrid(x, y)
plt.contourf(X, Y, f(X, Y), 8,
```

```
            alpha = 0.75, cmap='hot')
C = plt.contour(X, Y, f(X, Y), 8,
              colors='black')
plt.clabel(C, inline=1, fontsize=10)
plt.axis('off')
plt.show()
```

Figure 13-2 shows the output.

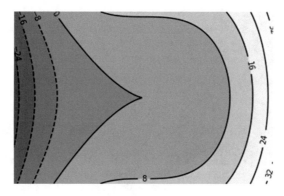

Figure 13-2. *Visualizing a function as a contour*

3D Vignettes

You can create a 3D vignette visualization as follows:

```
%matplotlib qt
fig = plt.figure()
ax = plt.axes(projection='3d')
X = np.arange(-4, 4, 0.25)
Y = np.arange(-4, 4, 0.25)
X, Y = np.meshgrid(X, Y)
R = np.sqrt(X ** 2 + Y ** 2)
Z = np.sin(R)
ax.plot_surface(X, Y, Z, rstride=1,
              cstride=1, cmap='hot')
ax.contourf(X, Y, Z, zdir='z',
          offset=-2, cmap='hot')
ax.set_zlim(-2, 2)
```

```
plt.axis('off')
ax.set_zticks(())
plt.show()
```

Figure 13-3 shows the output.

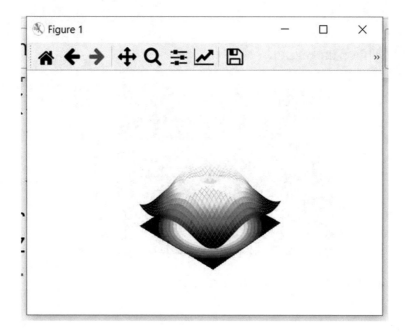

Figure 13-3. *Visualizing a 3D vignette*

Decorated Scatter Plots

You can create decorated scatter plots with Matplotlib. You need to pass the color and size as arguments. Here's an example:

```
%matplotlib inline
n = 1024
X = np.random.normal(0, 1, n)
Y = np.random.normal(0, 1, n)
color = np.arctan2(Y, X)
plt.scatter(X, Y, s=75, c=color, alpha=0.5)
plt.xlim(-1.5, 1.5)
```

```
plt.ylim(-1.5, 1.5)
plt.axis('off')
plt.show()
```

Figure 13-4 shows the output.

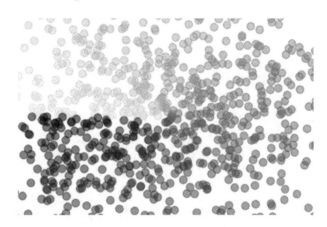

Figure 13-4. *Visualizing a decorated scatter plot*

Time Plots and Signals

You can visualize time plots and signals as follows:

```
N = 100
x = np.arange(N) # timestamps
y1 = np.random.randn(N)
y2 = np.random.randn(N)
y3 = np.random.randn(N)
y4 = np.random.randn(N)

plt.subplot(2, 1, 1)
plt.plot(x, y1)
plt.plot(x, y2, ':')
plt.grid()
plt.xlabel('Time')
plt.ylabel('y1 and y2')
plt.axis('tight')
plt.subplot(2, 1, 2)
```

```
plt.plot(x, y3)
plt.plot(x, y4, 'r')
plt.grid()
plt.xlabel('Time')
plt.ylabel('y3 and y4')
plt.axis('tight')
plt.show()
```

Figure 13-5 shows the output.

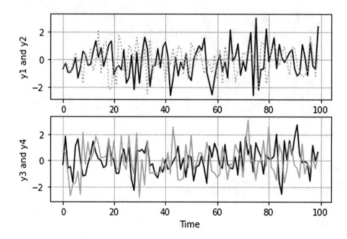

Figure 13-5. *Visualizing time plots and signals*

You can also multiply two signals. In the following code example, we are using the same x-axis to show all three graphs.

```
f = 1
t = np.arange( 0.0, 4.0, 0.01)
s1 = np.sin(2 *np.pi * f * t)
s2 = np.exp(-t)
s3 = s1 * s2
f = plt.figure()
plt.subplots_adjust(hspace=0.001)
ax1 = plt.subplot( 311 )
ax1.plot(t, s1)
plt.yticks(np.arange(-0.9, 1.0, 0.4))
plt.ylim(-1, 1)
```

```
ax2 = plt.subplot(312, sharex=ax1)
ax2.plot(t, s2)
plt.yticks(np.arange(0.1, 1.0, 0.2))
plt.ylim(0, 1)
ax3 = plt.subplot(313, sharex = ax1)
ax3.plot(t, s3)
plt.yticks(np.arange(-0.9, 1.0, 0.4))
plt.ylim(-1, 1)
xticklabels = ax1.get_xticklabels() + ax2.get_xticklabels()
plt.setp(xticklabels, visible=False)
plt.show()
```

Figure 13-6 shows the output.

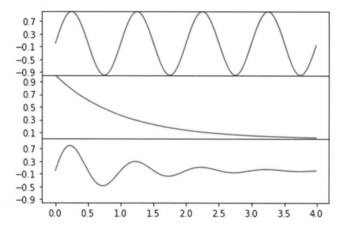

Figure 13-6. *Multiplying signals*

Filled Plots

You can fill in the empty spaces within the boundaries of plots as follows:

```
N = 1000
x = np.linspace(0, 1, N)
y = np.sin(4 * np.pi * x) + np.exp(-5 * x)
plt.fill(x, y, 'g', alpha = 0.8)
plt.grid(True)
plt.show()
```

Figure 13-7 shows the output.

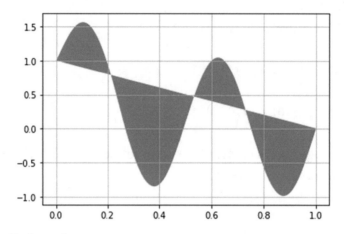

Figure 13-7. *Filled-in plots*

Step Plots

Let's visualize some sine waves first.

```
N = 100
x = np.linspace(-np.pi, np.pi, N)
y1 = 0.5 * np.sin(3*x)
y2 = 1.25 * np.sin(2*x)
y3 = 2 * np.sin(4*x)
plt.plot(x, y1, x, y2, x, y3)
plt.show()
```

Figure 13-8 shows the output.

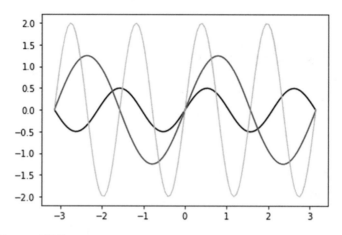

Figure 13-8. *Sinusoidals*

You can show them as step plots as follows:

```
plt.step(x, y1)
plt.step(x, y2)
plt.step(x, y3)
plt.show()
```

Figure 13-9 shows the output.

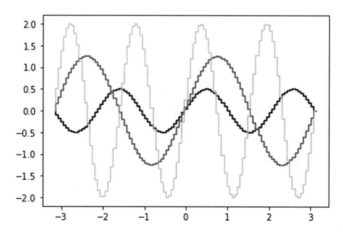

Figure 13-9. *Sinusoidals with step plots*

Hexbins

You can show data as hexbins as follows:

```
x, y = np.random.normal(size=(2, 10000))
plt.hexbin(x, y,
           gridsize=20,
           cmap='cool')
plt.colorbar()
plt.show()
```

Figure 13-10 shows the output.

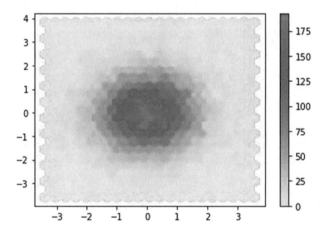

Figure 13-10. *Hexbin visualizations*

XKCD Style

You can visualize plots in the XKCD style. The XKCD is a popular a web comic. `https://xkcd.com` is the homepage of the web comic.

```
y = np.random.randn(1000)
plt.xkcd()
plt.hist(y)
plt.show()
```

Figure 13-11 shows the output.

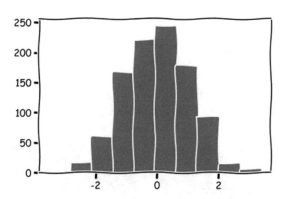

Figure 13-11. *XKCD histogram*

Another example is as follows:

```
y = np.random.randn(1000)
plt.xkcd()
plt.hist(y, bins = 30,
        range=[-3.5, 3.5],
        facecolor='r',
        alpha=0.6,
        edgecolor='k')
plt.grid()
plt.show()
```

Figure 13-12 shows the output.

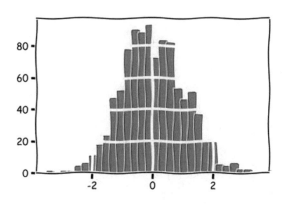

Figure 13-12. *Another XKCD histogram*

You can visualize 2D histograms too in the same way, as shown here:

```
data = np.random.randn(1000, 1000)
plt.xkcd()
plt.hist2d(data[0], data[1])
plt.show()
```

Figure 13-13 shows the output.

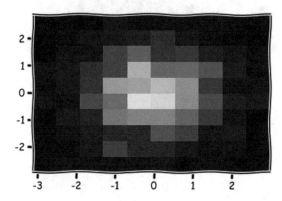

Figure 13-13. *A third XKCD histogram*

Summary

In this chapter, you learned how to work with some additional visualization techniques using Matplotlib.

In the next chapter, you will get acquainted with a data science library known as Pandas.

CHAPTER 14

Introduction to Pandas

In the previous chapter, you learned many Matplotlib techniques. You will now learn how to use another library that is common in data science and data visualization.

In this chapter, we will be focusing on the basics of the main data science and analytics library in the scientific Python ecosystem: Pandas. You will learn about the data structures in this library. The following are the topics in the chapter:

- Introduction to Pandas

- Series in Pandas

- Dataframe in Pandas

After reading this chapter, you will be comfortable doing basic tasks with Pandas.

Introduction to Pandas

Pandas is a data analytics component in the scientific Python ecosystem. In fact, it is an integral part of the scientific Python ecosystem. It comes with versatile data structures and routines to manage them. It comes with versatile data structures and routines to manage those data structures.

Let's install Pandas on a computer by running the following command in Jupyter Notebook:

```
!pip3 install pandas
```

You can import it to the current session by running the following commands:

```
import pandas as pd
```

You can read more about Pandas at `https://pandas.pydata.org/`.

© Ashwin Pajankar 2022
A. Pajankar, *Hands-on Matplotlib*, https://doi.org/10.1007/978-1-4842-7410-1_14

Series in Pandas

A series is a one-dimensional array with labels. It can hold data of any type. The labels are collectively known as the *index*.

You can create a series as follows:

```
s1 = pd.Series([3, 2, 1 , 75, -3.14])
```

You can check its datatypes as follows:

```
type(s1)
```

The following is the output:

```
<class 'pandas.core.series.Series'>
```

You can see the values and index associated with the data as follows:

```
print(s1)
```

The following is the output:

```
0       3.00
1       2.00
2       1.00
3      75.00
4      -3.14
dtype: float64
```

You can explicitly mention the datatype as follows:

```
s2 = pd.Series([3, 2, 1 , 75, -3.14], dtype=np.float32)
print(s2)
```

You can pass a list as an argument to the constructor function to create a series, as follows:

```
x = [3, 2, 1 , 75, -3.14]
s3 = pd.Series(x)
```

You can even pass a NumPy Ndarray as an argument to the constructor function to create a series, as follows:

```
import numpy as np
y = np.array(x)
s4 = pd.Series(y)
```

You can see the values as follows:

```
print(s4.values)
```

The following is the output:

```
[ 3.    2.    1.    75.    -3.14]
```

You can retrieve the index as follows:

```
print(s4.index)
```

The output is as follows:

```
RangeIndex(start=0, stop=5, step=1)
```

You can assign a custom index as follows:

```
s5 = pd.Series( x, index = ['a', 'b', 'c', 'd', 'e'])
print(s5)
```

The output is as follows:

```
a       3.00
b       2.00
c       1.00
d       75.00
e       -3.14
dtype: float64
```

Basic Operations on Series

You can perform a few basic operations on a series. For example, you can display the negative numbers as follows:

```
print(s5[s5 < 0])
```

The output is as follows:

```
e    -3.14
dtype: float64
```

You can retrieve the positive numbers as follows:

```
print(s5[s5 > 0])
```

The output is as follows:

```
a     3.0
b     2.0
c     1.0
d    75.0
dtype: float64
```

These were examples of a comparison operation. You can perform arithmetic operations such as multiplication as follows:

```
c = 3
print ( s5 * c )
```

The output is as follows:

```
a      9.00
b      6.00
c      3.00
d    225.00
e     -9.42
dtype: float64
```

Dataframe in Pandas

A dataframe is a two-dimensional labeled data structure with columns that can be different datatypes. You can create dataframes from series, Ndarrys, lists, and dictionaries.

Dataframes have labels, which are collectively called an *index*. You can easily view and manipulate the data in the dataframes. The data is stored in a rectangular grid format in dataframes.

You can create a dataframe from a list as follows. The following is a dictionary:

```
data = {'city': ['Delhi', 'Delhi', 'Delhi',
                 'Bangalore', 'Bangalore', 'Bangalore'],
        'year': [2020, 2021, 2022, 2020, 2021, 2022,],
        'population': [10.0, 10.1, 10.2, 5.2, 5.3, 5.5]}
```

Let's create a dataframe from this, as shown here:

```
df1 = pd.DataFrame(data)
print(df1)
```

The output is as follows:

```
        city  year  population
0      Delhi  2020        10.0
1      Delhi  2021        10.1
2      Delhi  2022        10.2
3  Bangalore  2020         5.2
4  Bangalore  2021         5.3
5  Bangalore  2022         5.5
```

You can see the top five records as follows:

```
df1.head()
```

The output is as follows:

```
     city  year  population
0   Delhi  2020        10.0
1   Delhi  2021        10.1
2   Delhi  2022        10.2
```

```
3  Bangalore  2020       5.2
4  Bangalore  2021       5.3
```

You can also pass other numbers as arguments to the function head(), and it will show that many top records from the dataframe. Similarly, you can use df1.tail() to see the last records. It also has 5 as the default argument, but you can customize the argument passed to it.

You can create a dataframe with a particular order of columns as follows:

```
df2 = pd.DataFrame(data, columns=['year', 'city', 'population'])
print(df2)
```

The output is as follows:

```
   year        city  population
0  2020       Delhi        10.0
1  2021       Delhi        10.1
2  2022       Delhi        10.2
3  2020   Bangalore         5.2
4  2021   Bangalore         5.3
5  2022   Bangalore         5.5
```

Let's create a dataframe with an additional column and custom index as follows:

```
df3 = pd.DataFrame(data, columns=['year', 'city', 'population', 'GDP'],
                   index = ['one', 'two', 'three', 'four', 'five', 'six'])
print(df3)
```

The following is the new dataframe:

```
       year        city  population  GDP
one    2020       Delhi        10.0  NaN
two    2021       Delhi        10.1  NaN
three  2022       Delhi        10.2  NaN
four   2020   Bangalore         5.2  NaN
five   2021   Bangalore         5.3  NaN
six    2022   Bangalore         5.5  NaN
```

You can print the list of columns as follows:

```
print(df3.columns)
```

The output is as follows:

```
Index(['year', 'city', 'population', 'GDP'], dtype='object')
```

You can print the list of indexes as follows:

```
print(df3.index)
```

The output is as follows:

```
Index(['one', 'two', 'three', 'four', 'five', 'six'], dtype='object')
```

You can see the data of a column with the following statement:

```
print(df3.year)
```

or you can also use the following statement:

```
print(df3['year'])
```

The following is the output:

```
one        2020
two        2021
three      2022
four       2020
five       2021
six        2022
Name: year, dtype: int64
```

You can see the datatype of a column with the following statement:

```
print(df3['year'].dtype)
```

or you can use the following:

```
print(df3.year.dtype)
```

The output is as follows:

```
int64
```

You can see the datatype of all the columns as follows:

```
print(df3.dtypes)
```

The output is as follows:

```
year              int64
city             object
population       float64
GDP              object
dtype: object
```

You can retrieve any record using the index as follows:

```
df3.loc['one']
```

The output is as follows:

```
year             2020
city             Delhi
population       10.0
GDP              NaN
Name: one, dtype: object
```

You can assign the same value to all the members of a column as follows:

```
df3.GDP = 10
print(df3)
```

The output is as follows:

```
        year       city  population  GDP
one     2020      Delhi        10.0   10
two     2021      Delhi        10.1   10
three   2022      Delhi        10.2   10
four    2020  Bangalore         5.2   10
five    2021  Bangalore         5.3   10
six     2022  Bangalore         5.5   10
```

You can assign an Ndarray to the column GDP as follows:

```
import numpy as np
df3.GDP = np.arange(6)
print(df3)
```

The output is as follows:

```
        year       city  population  GDP
one     2020      Delhi        10.0    0
two     2021      Delhi        10.1    1
three   2022      Delhi        10.2    2
four    2020  Bangalore         5.2    3
five    2021  Bangalore         5.3    4
six     2022  Bangalore         5.5    5
```

You can also assign it a list as follows:

```
df3.GDP = [3, 2, 0, 9, -0.4, 7]
print(df3)
```

The output is as follows:

```
        year       city  population  GDP
one     2020      Delhi        10.0  3.0
two     2021      Delhi        10.1  2.0
three   2022      Delhi        10.2  0.0
four    2020  Bangalore         5.2  9.0
five    2021  Bangalore         5.3 -0.4
six     2022  Bangalore         5.5  7.0
```

Let's assign a series to it as follows:

```
val = pd.Series([-1.4, 1.5, -1.3], index=['two', 'four', 'five'])
df3.GDP = val
print(df3)
```

The output is as follows:

```
        year       city  population  GDP
one     2020      Delhi        10.0  NaN
two     2021      Delhi        10.1 -1.4
three   2022      Delhi        10.2  NaN
four    2020  Bangalore         5.2  1.5
five    2021  Bangalore         5.3 -1.3
six     2022  Bangalore         5.5  NaN
```

Summary

In this chapter, you explored the basics of the Pandas data science library of the scientific Python ecosystem. You learned the basics of creating and using the fundamental Pandas data structures, which are the series and dataframe.

In the next chapter, you will learn how to programmatically read the data stored in various formats using the libraries NumPy, Pandas, and Matplotlib.

CHAPTER 15

Data Acquisition

In the previous chapter, you learned the basics of using two Pandas data structures, namely, the series and the dataframe.

This chapter focuses on acquiring data with Python using all the libraries you have studied up to now (NumPy, Matplotlib, and Pandas). The following are the topics you will learn about in this chapter:

- Handling plain-text files

- Handling CSV files with Python

- Using Python and Excel

- Writing and reading files with NumPy

- Reading data from a CSV file with NumPy

- Using a Matplotlib CBook

- Reading data from a CSV file

- Reading data from an Excel file

- Reading data from a JSON file

- Reading data from a Pickle file

- Reading data from the Web

- Reading data from a relational database

- Reading data from the clipboard

After reading this chapter, you will be comfortable reading data from various file formats and saving it.

© Ashwin Pajankar 2022
A. Pajankar, *Hands-on Matplotlib*, https://doi.org/10.1007/978-1-4842-7410-1_15

Plain-Text File Handling

Let's learn how to read data from and write data to a plain-text file. Python comes with the functionality to read and write plain-text files. We have four modes for opening a file, as listed here:

- w: Write

- r: Read

- a: Append

- r+: Read and write mode

You can use them (one at a time) as follows:

```
f = open('testfile.txt', 'w')
print(f)
```

This code opens the testfile.txt file in write mode. If the file does not exist, then Python creates this file in the current location on disk. If the file already exists, it overwrites the contents of the file. The previous code prints the file object as follows:

```
<_io.TextIOWrapper name='testfile.txt' mode='w' encoding='cp1252'>
```

Let's write some data to the file. In this case, the data consists of multicharacter strings.

```
f.write('This is a test string.\n')
f.write('This is the middle line.\n')
f.write('This is the last line.')
```

You can close the file object (also called the *file handle*) as follows:

```
f.close()
```

You know that opening a file again in write mode will overwrite its data. So, this time, let's open the same file in append mode as follows:

```
f = open('testfile.txt', 'a')
f.write('\nThis is the appended line.')
f.close()
```

We are writing one line into the file and then closing the file. Let's read the data and print it as follows:

```
f = open('testfile.txt', 'r')
print(f.read())
f.close()
```

The output is as follows:

```
This is a test string.
This is the middle line.
This is the last line.
This is the appended line
```

You can retrieve the lines in a list (with every line in the file corresponding to an element in the list), as follows:

```
f = open('testfile.txt', 'r')
print(f.readlines())
f.close()
```

The output is as follows:

```
['This is a test string.\n', 'This is the middle line.\n', 'This is the
last line.\n', 'This is the appended line.']
```

You can also retrieve the data in the file line by line as follows:

```
f = open('testfile.txt', 'r')
for line in f:
    print(line)
f.close()
```

The output is as follows:

```
This is a test string.

This is the middle line.

This is the last line.

This is the appended line.
```

Handling CSV Files with Python

Let's learn a few things about the comma-separated file (CSV) format. CSV files store data in plain-text format, and the data items are either a fixed length or separated by a delimiter such as a comma (,), a pipe (|), or a colon(:). The most common CSV format uses a comma as the delimiter, and many times the first line is used to store the names of the columns.

In this section, you will learn how to handle a CSV file with Python 3. Python 3 comes with a built-in library to handle CSV files. You do not have to install anything. You can import the library as follows:

```
import csv
```

You can open the file as a plain-text file in read mode as follows:

```
file = open('test.csv', 'r')
print(file)
```

Once you open the file, you can pass the file handle to the routine `csv.reader()` as follows:

```
csvfile = csv.reader(file, delimiter=',')
print(csvfile)
```

This prints the value of the object as follows:

```
<_csv.reader object at 0x0590AC68>
```

You can retrieve the data line by line as follows:

```
for row in csvfile:
    print(row)
```

This produces the following output:

```
['Banana', 'Yellow', '250']
['Orange', 'Orange', '200']
['Grapes', 'Green', '400']
['Tomato', 'Red', '100']
['Spinach', 'Green', '40']
['Potatoes', 'Gray', '400']
```

```
['Rice', 'White', '300']
['Rice', 'Brown', '400']
['Wheat', 'Brown', '500']
['Barley', 'Yellow', '500']
```

You can display the elements individually as follows:

```
for row in csvfile:
    for element in row:
        print(element)
```

The output is as follows:

```
Banana
Yellow
250
Orange
Orange
200
Grapes
Green
400
Tomato
Red
100
Spinach
Green
40
Potatoes
Gray
400
Rice
White
300
Rice
Brown
400
```

```
Wheat
Brown
500
Barley
Yellow
500
```

Let's close the file handle as follows:

```
file.close()
```

Python and Excel

Let's see how to read the data from Excel. You need an external library for that. The following code installs the library that we will use in this section:

```
!pip3 install openpyxl
```

You can import it as follows:

```
import openpyxl
```

You can open an Excel file as follows:

```
wb = openpyxl.load_workbook('test.xlsx')
print(wb)
print(type(wb))
```

The output is as follows:

```
<openpyxl.workbook.workbook.Workbook object at 0x0E87F7D8>
<class 'openpyxl.workbook.workbook.Workbook'>
```

You can retrieve the names of all the sheets as follows:

```
print(wb.sheetnames)
```

The output is as follows:

```
['Sheet1', 'Sheet2', 'Sheet3']
```

You can select a sheet as follows:

```
currSheet = wb['Sheet1']
print(currSheet)
print(type(currSheet))
```

The output is as follows:

```
<Worksheet "Sheet1">
<class 'openpyxl.worksheet.worksheet.Worksheet'>
```

Similarly, the following code has the same effect:

```
currSheet = wb[wb.sheetnames[0]]
print(currSheet)
print(type(currSheet))
```

You can print the name of the current sheet as follows:

```
print(currSheet.title)
```

The output is as follows:

```
Sheet1
```

You can print the value of a cell as follows:

```
var1 = currSheet['A1']
print(var1.value)
```

The output is as follows:

```
Food Item
```

The other way to do the same activity is as follows:

```
print(currSheet['B1'].value)
```

You can do this another way as follows:

```
var2 = currSheet.cell(row=2, column=2)
print(var2.value)
```

The number of rows and columns can be obtained as follows:

```
print(currSheet.max_row)
print(currSheet.max_column)
```

The output is as follows:

```
11
3
```

Let's print all the data in the spreadsheet as follows:

```
for i in range(currSheet.max_row):
    print('---Beginning of Row---')
    for j in range(currSheet.max_column):
        var = currSheet.cell(row=i+1, column=j+1)
        print(var.value)
    print('---End of Row---')
```

The output is very long, so I've truncated it here. Please run the code to see it for yourself.

Writing and Reading Files with NumPy

Let's see how to read and write files with NumPy. Let's create a dataset with NumPy as follows:

```
import numpy as np
x = np.arange(100)
print(x)
```

The output is as follows:

```
[ 0  1  2  3  4  5  6  7  8  9 10 11 12 13 14 15 16 17 18 19 20 21 22 23
 24 25 26 27 28 29 30 31 32 33 34 35 36 37 38 39 40 41 42 43 44 45 46 47
 48 49 50 51 52 53 54 55 56 57 58 59 60 61 62 63 64 65 66 67 68 69 70 71
 72 73 74 75 76 77 78 79 80 81 82 83 84 85 86 87 88 89 90 91 92 93 94 95
 96 97 98 99]
```

You can save it to a file (in NumPy data format) as follows:

```
np.save('test.npy', x)
```

You can load the data from a file into a variable as follows:

```
data = np.load('test.npy')
print(data)
```

The output is as follows:

```
[ 0  1  2  3  4  5  6  7  8  9 10 11 12 13 14 15 16 17 18 19 20 21 22 23
 24 25 26 27 28 29 30 31 32 33 34 35 36 37 38 39 40 41 42 43 44 45 46 47
 48 49 50 51 52 53 54 55 56 57 58 59 60 61 62 63 64 65 66 67 68 69 70 71
 72 73 74 75 76 77 78 79 80 81 82 83 84 85 86 87 88 89 90 91 92 93 94 95
 96 97 98 99]
```

Reading the Data from a CSV File with NumPy

The CSV file can be read with NumPy too as follows:

```
import numpy as np
# Reads only numeric data
data = np.loadtxt('data.csv', delimiter=',')
print(data)
```

The output is as follows:

```
[[  0.    1.   18.    2.]
 [  1.    6.    1.    3.]
 [  2.    3.  154.    0.]
 [  4.  978.    3.    6.]
 [  5.    2.   41.   45.]
 [  6.   67.    2.    3.]
 [  7.    5.   67.    2.]]
```

You can also skip rows and columns as follows:

```
data = np.loadtxt('data.csv', delimiter=',',
                skiprows=3, usecols=[1, 3])
print(data)
```

The output is as follows:

```
[[978.    6.]
 [  2.   45.]
 [ 67.    3.]
 [  5.    2.]]
```

Matplotlib CBook

You can read data that is stored in Matplotlib's CBook format. Matplotlib comes with a few sample files in that format. Let's see how to read the data:

```
import matplotlib.cbook as cbook
datafile = cbook.get_sample_data('aapl.npz')
r = np.load(datafile)
print(r.files)
```

This will print the names of the data files, as shown here:

```
['price_data']
```

Let's read the data from that data file:

```
print(r['price_data'])
```

This shows the Apple share price data as follows:

```
[('1984-09-07',  26.5 ,  26.87,  26.25,  26.5 ,  2981600,   3.02)
 ('1984-09-10',  26.5 ,  26.62,  25.87,  26.37,  2346400,   3.01)
 ('1984-09-11',  26.62,  27.37,  26.62,  26.87,  5444000,   3.07) ...
 ('2008-10-10',  85.7 , 100.  ,  85.  ,  96.8 , 79260700,  96.8 )
 ('2008-10-13', 104.55, 110.53, 101.02, 110.26, 54967000, 110.26)
 ('2008-10-14', 116.26, 116.4 , 103.14, 104.08, 70749800, 104.08)]
```

Reading Data from a CSV

As mentioned earlier, a CSV file contains values separated by commas. You can use the versatile function read_csv() in Pandas to read a CSV file on the Web or on the local/networked disk. The following are the contents of a CSV file that we will use in this demonstration:

```
rank,discipline,phd,service,sex,salary
Prof,B,56,49,Male,186960
Prof,A,12,6,Male,93000
Prof,A,23,20,Male,110515
Prof,A,40,31,Male,131205
Prof,B,20,18,Male,104800
Prof,A,20,20,Male,122400
AssocProf,A,20,17,Male,81285
```

The first row is the header row. Most CSV files will have a header row, although it is not required. As you can see, the values are separated by commas. This is a common format of CSV files. Depending on the system and application, you can use a variety of separators like a space, a semicolon (;), or a pipe (|). Also, CSV files can use a fixed number of characters for storing data in columns. In this example, as discussed, we are using one of the most common CSV formats for storing data.

Let's learn how to read data from such files with Pandas. Create a new notebook for this chapter.

Import the Pandas library as follows:

```
import pandas as pd
```

Let's read a CSV file located on the Web as follows:

```
df1 = pd.read_csv("http://rcs.bu.edu/examples/python/data_analysis/
Salaries.csv")
print(df1)
```

You can also read a CSV stored on the local disk as follows:

```
df2 = pd.read_csv("Salaries.csv")
print(df2)
```

You can also dump the data of a dataframe to a CSV file at a disk location as follows:

```
df2.to_csv('output.csv', index=True, header=False)
```

The code will create a CSV file on the disk in the current directory.

Reading Data from an Excel File

To read data from an Excel file into a Pandas dataframe, you need the support of an external package. Let's install a package as follows:

```
!pip3 install xlrd
```

Now let's read the Excel file stored on the disk, as follows:

```
excel_file = 'test.xlsx'
df1 = pd.read_excel(excel_file)
```

Here (and in the earlier example too), the file is stored in the same directory as the notebook file. If you need to read the file in any other location, you must specify the full path of that file. The previous code, when executed, will load the contents of an Excel file into a Pandas dataframe. You can see the contents using the following line of code:

```
print(df1)
```

Figure 15-1 shows the output.

	Fruit	Color	Weight
0	Banana	Yellow	250
1	Orange	Orange	200
2	Grapes	Green	400
3	Tomato	Red	100
4	Spinach	Green	40
5	Potatoes	Gray	400
6	Rice	White	300
7	Rice	Brown	400
8	Wheat	Brown	500
9	Barley	Yellow	500

Figure 15-1. *The data from an Excel sheet*

Reading Data from JSON

You can read the data of a JSON string into a dataframe as follows. Create a JSON string first.

```
obj = """
{"name": "Ashwin",
"places_lived": ["Nashik", "Hyderabad", "Bangalore"],
"pet": null,
"siblings": [{"name": "Scott", "age": 30, "pets": ["Zeus", "Zuko"]},
{"name": "Katie", "age": 38,
"pets": ["Sixes", "Stache", "Cisco"]}]
}
"""
```

You can print the string as follows:

```
print(obj)
```

You can also check the type of the variable (it is a string in JSON format), as shown here:

```
print(type(obj))
```

You can convert this JSON-formatted string to a dictionary as follows:

```
import json
result = json.loads(obj)
print(result)
```

Let's check the data type of the newly created variable, as shown here:

```
print(type(result))
```

This will produce the following result:

```
<class 'dict'>
```

Let's load the data into a dataframe as follows:

```
df1 = pd.DataFrame(result['siblings'], columns=['name', 'age'])
print(df1)
```

The output is as follows:

```
    name   age
0   Scott   30
1   Katie   38
```

You can also read the data from a JSON file as follows:

```
df2 = pd.read_json('example_2.json')
print(df2)
```

This is how you can read the JSON data into dataframes.

Reading Data from a Pickle File

In Python programming, Pickle is used in serializing and deserializing Python Objects. You can store a Pandas dataframe to a Pickle file on the disk as follows:

```
data = [1, 2, 3, 4, 5]
df1 = pd.DataFrame(data)
print(df1)
df1.to_pickle('mypickle')
```

You can read the data from a Pickle file stored on the disk as follows:

```
df2 = pd.read_pickle('mypickle')
print(df2)
```

Reading Data from the Web

Let's read the data from the Web. For that, you will need a few libraries. You can install them as follows:

```
!pip3 install lxml html5lib BeautifulSoup4
```

You can read an HTML file located on the Web as follows:

```
df1 = pd.read_html('https://www.google.com/')
```

Let's get the details of the object and the data as follows:

```
print(df1)
len(df1)
type(df1)
df1[0].head()
```

You can also parse this retrieved HTML text and fetch important information from the tags as follows:

```
from lxml import objectify
from io import StringIO
```

The following is an HTML tag string and a way to parse it, as shown here:

```
tag = '<a href="http://www.google.com/">Google</a>'
root = objectify.parse(StringIO(tag)).getroot()
```

You retrieve the root and the text of this object as follows:

```
print(root)
root.get('href')
print(root.text)
```

This will produce the following output:

```
Google
Google
```

Interacting with the Web API

Let's learn to interact with the web API to retrieve and store the data into a Pandas dataframe. Install the necessary library as follows:

```
!pip3 install requests
```

Let's import the library as follows:

```
import requests
```

Let's create a URL string as follows:

```
url='https://api.github.com/repos/pandas-dev/pandas/issues'
```

You can fetch the data from the URL with the HTTP GET request issued programmatically as follows:

```
resp = requests.get(url)
```

You can check the response code and its datatype as follows:

```
print(resp)
print(type(resp))
```

The output is as follows:

```
<Response [200]>
<class 'requests.models.Response'>
```

The HTTP response code 200 stands for success in retrieving the information. You can retrieve the actual information as follows:

```
data = resp.json()
print(type(data))
```

It will be a list, as shown here:

```
<class 'list'>
```

You can convert it into a dataframe as follows:

```
output = pd.DataFrame(data, columns=['number', 'title', 'labels', 'state'])
print(output)
```

Figure 15-2 shows the output.

	number	title	labels	state
0	40650	DOC: Update CSS alignment for main documentati...	[{'id': 134699, 'node_id': 'MDU6TGFiZWwxMzQ2OT...	open
1	40649	BUG: read_excel failed with empty rows after M...	[{'id': 76811, 'node_id': 'MDU6TGFiZWw3NjgxMQ=...	open
2	40647	ENH: df.to_sql lacks a parameter if_not_exist...	[{'id': 76812, 'node_id': 'MDU6TGFiZWw3NjgxMg=...	open
3	40646	BUG:	[{'id': 76811, 'node_id': 'MDU6TGFiZWw3NjgxMQ=...	open
4	40645	DOC: Styling guide lacks links to the referenc...	[{'id': 134699, 'node_id': 'MDU6TGFiZWwxMzQ2OT...	open
5	40644	DOC: Change user guide style notebook to reST	[]	open
6	40642	TYP: IndexOpsMixin	[{'id': 1280988427, 'node_id': 'MDU6TGFiZWwxMj...	open

Figure 15-2. *The data from an HTTPS GET response*

This is how you can work with data available on the Web.

Reading Data from a Relational Database Table

You can read the data stored in a table in a relational database like MySQL or MariaDB. You can read more about the installation and usage at the following URLs:

```
https://www.mysql.com/
https://mariadb.org/
```

You have to install an external library as follows:

```
!pip3 install pymysql
```

Then you need to import the library to the notebook as follows:

```
import pymysql
```

You can connect to a MySQL or MariaDB database instance as follows:

```
db = pymysql.connect(host="localhost", user="root",
                     password="test123", database="world")
```

Then you can read the output of a SELECT query into a dataframe as follows:

```
df1 = pd.read_sql('select * from country', db)
print(df1)
```

This produces the output shown in Figure 15-3.

	Code	Name	Continent	Region	SurfaceArea	IndepYear	Population
0	ABW	Aruba	North America	Caribbean	193.0	NaN	103000
1	AFG	Afghanistan	Asia	Southern and Central Asia	652090.0	1919.0	22720000
2	AGO	Angola	Africa	Central Africa	1246700.0	1975.0	12878000
3	AIA	Anguilla	North America	Caribbean	96.0	NaN	8000
4	ALB	Albania	Europe	Southern Europe	28748.0	1912.0	3401200
5	AND	Andorra	Europe	Southern Europe	468.0	1278.0	78000

Figure 15-3. *The data from a MySQL/MariaDB table*

Reading Data from the Clipboard

You can read the data stored on the clipboard. The clipboard is a temporary and unnamed buffer in the computer's main memory (RAM) that a few operating systems provide for the short-term storage and transfer of data within and between programs. For example, whenever you copy text data from a file, it is stored on the clipboard of the operating system.

Copy the following data into your computer's clipboard by selecting it and pressing the Ctrl+C buttons on the keyboard.

```
  A B C
x 1 2 a
y 2 3 b
z 3 4 c
```

You can load it into a Pandas dataframe using the following code:

```
df = pd.read_clipboard()
```

You can also copy data onto the clipboard programmatically as follows:

```
import numpy as np
df = pd.DataFrame(np.random.randn(5, 3))
df.to_clipboard()
```

You can see this data either by reading the clipboard programmatically into a dataframe as explained earlier or by pasting it with the Ctrl+V command into a text editor like Notepad (on Windows) or Leafpad or gedit (on Linux).

Summary

In this chapter, you learned how to read data from multiple file formats and how to load that data into Python variables.

In the next chapter, you will study how to visualize Pandas data using Matplotlib.

CHAPTER 16

Visualizing Data with Pandas and Matplotlib

In the previous chapter, you learned how to read the data stored in various file formats into Python variables using NumPy, Pandas, and Matplotlib.

You should be comfortable working with data now. In this chapter, you will practice writing programs related to another important and practical aspect of the field of data science: dataset visualization. This chapter contains lots of examples of short code snippets to demonstrate how to create visualizations of datasets. So, let's continue our journey of data science with the following topics in this chapter:

- Simple plots

- Bar graphs

- Histograms

- Box plots

- Area plots

- Scatter plots

- Hexagonal bin plots

- Pie charts

After this chapter, you will be able to create impressive visualizations of datasets with Pandas and Matplotlib.

© Ashwin Pajankar 2022

A. Pajankar, *Hands-on Matplotlib*, https://doi.org/10.1007/978-1-4842-7410-1_16

Simple Plots

Let's jump directly into the hands-on examples for data visualization. You will learn how to visualize simple plots first. I recommend you create a new notebook for the code examples in this chapter.

Let's start with the magical command that imports all the required libraries, as follows:

```
%matplotlib inline
import matplotlib.pyplot as plt
import pandas as pd
import numpy as np
```

Let's create some data using the routine cumsum(), as follows:

```
df1 = pd.DataFrame(np.random.randn(100, 2), columns=['B', 'C']).cumsum()
df1['A'] = pd.Series(list(range(100)))
print(df1)
```

The resultant dataset will have three columns, as follows:

```
           B          C    A
0   -0.684779  -0.655677    0
1   -0.699163  -1.868611    1
2   -0.315527  -3.513103    2
3   -0.504069  -4.175940    3
4    0.998419  -4.385832    4
..        ...        ...   ..
95   1.149399  -1.445029   95
96   2.035029  -1.886731   96
97   0.938699   0.188980   97
98   2.449148   0.335828   98
99   2.204369  -1.304379   99

[100 rows x 3 columns]
```

Let's use the routine plot() to visualize this data. The plot() routine that the dataframe object uses calls Pyplot's plot() by default. Here's an example:

```
plt.figure()
df1.plot(x='A', y='B')
plt.show()
```

This code is self-explanatory. We are passing strings that contain the names of columns as arguments for the x- and y-axes. It produces the output depicted in Figure 16-1.

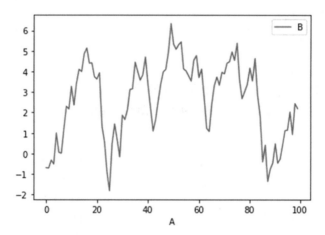

Figure 16-1. *Visualizing a simple plot*

You can use other columns in the visualization as well, as shown here:

```
plt.figure()
df1.plot(x='A', y='C')
plt.show()
```

Run this example to see the result. This is how you can use different combinations of columns to visualize data.

Bar Graphs

Let's create a simple bar graph using the same dataset. Let's pick a record from this dataframe as follows:

```
print(df1.iloc[4])
```

The following is the output:

```
B    0.998419
C    -4.385832
A    4.000000
Name: 4, dtype: float64
```

Let's draw a simple bar graph with this data using the routine bar(). The following is the code snippet for that:

```
plt.figure()
df1.iloc[4].plot.bar()
plt.axhline(0, color='k')
plt.show()
```

In this code example, we are using axhline() to draw a horizontal line corresponding to the x-axis. Figure 16-2 shows the output.

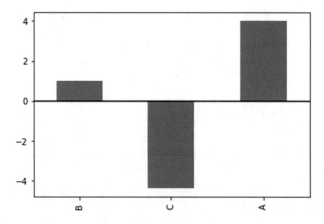

Figure 16-2. *Visualizing a simple bar graph*

Let's discuss a more complex example of a bar graph. Let's create a new dataset as follows:

```
df2 = pd.DataFrame(np.random.rand(10, 4), columns=['a', 'b', 'c', 'd'])
print(df2)
```

The output is as follows:

	a	b	c	d
0	0.352173	0.127452	0.637665	0.734944
1	0.375190	0.931818	0.769403	0.927441
2	0.830744	0.942059	0.781032	0.557774
3	0.977058	0.594992	0.557016	0.862058
4	0.960796	0.329448	0.493713	0.971139
5	0.364460	0.516401	0.432365	0.587528
6	0.292020	0.500945	0.889294	0.211502
7	0.770808	0.519468	0.279582	0.419549
8	0.982924	0.458197	0.938682	0.123614
9	0.578290	0.186395	0.901216	0.099061

In the earlier example, we visualized only a single row. Now, let's visualize the entire dataset as follows:

```
plt.figure()
df2.plot.bar()
plt.show()
```

This will create a bar graph for every row. The graphs will be grouped together per the rows, as shown in Figure 16-3.

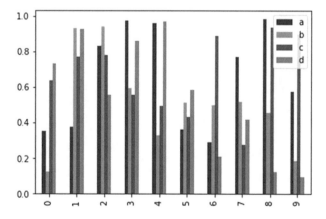

Figure 16-3. *Visualizing a more complex bar graph*

You can see that the indices are represented on the x-axis, and magnitudes are marked on the y-axis. This is an unstacked vertical bar graph. You can create a stacked variation of it by just passing a simple argument as follows:

```
plt.figure()
df2.plot.bar(stacked=True)
plt.show()
```

Figure 16-4 shows the output.

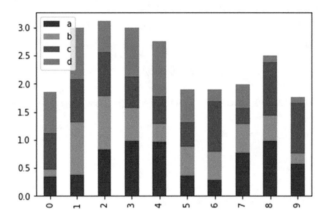

Figure 16-4. *Visualizing vertically stacked bar graphs*

You can even create horizontal stacked and unstacked bar graphs too. Let's create a horizontally stacked bar graph with the routine barh() as follows:

```
plt.figure()
df2.plot.barh(stacked=True)
plt.show()
```

Figure 16-5 shows the output.

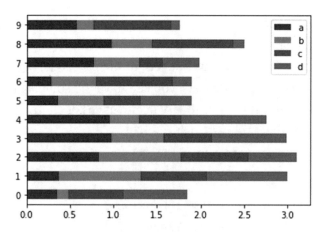

Figure 16-5. *Visualizing horizontally stacked bar graphs*

Let's write a code snippet for an unstacked horizontal bar graph by omitting the argument as follows:

```
plt.figure()
df2.plot.barh()
plt.show()
```

Figure 16-6 shows the output.

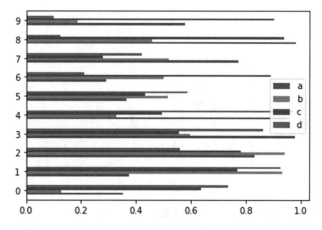

Figure 16-6. *Visualizing horizontal unstacked bar graphs*

You've just learned how to create various types of bar graphs.

217

Histograms

A histogram is a visual representation of the frequency distribution of numerical data. It was first used by Karl Pearson.

We first divide the data into various buckets, or bins. The size of the bins depends on the requirements. For integer datasets, you can have the smallest bin size, which is 1. Then for each bin, you can list the number of occurrences of elements that fall under the bin. Then you can show that table as a bar graph.

You can draw the histogram of a given dataset with Pandas and Matplotlib. Let's create a dataset as follows:

```
df4 = pd.DataFrame({'a': np.random.randn(1000) + 1,
                    'b': np.random.randn(1000),
                    'c': np.random.randn(1000) - 1},
                   columns=['a', 'b', 'c'])
print(df4)
```

The generated dataset is as follows:

```
            a         b         c
0    1.454474 -0.517940 -0.772909
1    1.886328  0.868393  0.109613
2    0.041313 -1.959168 -0.713575
3    0.650075  0.457937 -0.501023
4    1.684392 -0.072837  1.821190
..        ...       ...       ...
995  0.800481 -1.209032 -0.249132
996  0.490104  0.253966 -1.185503
997  2.304285  0.082134 -1.068881
998  1.249055  0.040750 -0.488890
999 -1.216627  0.444629 -1.198375

[1000 rows x 3 columns]
```

Let's visualize this dataset as a histogram using the routine hist(), as follows:

```
plt.figure();
df4.plot.hist(alpha=0.7)
plt.show()
```

Figure 16-7 shows the output.

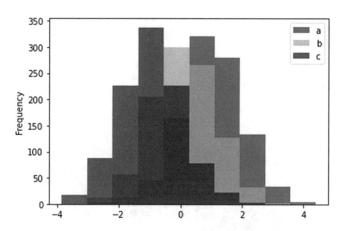

Figure 16-7. *Visualizing a dataset as a histogram*

The argument passed to routine decides the opacity (or alpha transparency) of the output. You had to make this transparent in the previous example because the histogram was unstacked. Let's create a stacked histogram with the size of the buckets as 20, as follows:

```
plt.figure();
df4.plot.hist(stacked=True, bins=20)
plt.show()
```

Figure 16-8 shows the output.

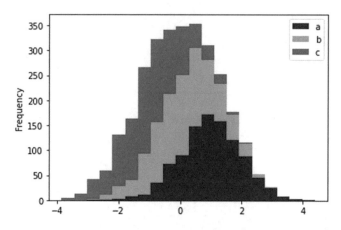

Figure 16-8. *Visualizing the same dataset as an unstacked histogram*

Let's create a horizontal cumulative histogram of a single column as follows:

```
plt.figure();
df4['a'].plot.hist(orientation='horizontal', cumulative=True)
plt.show()
```

Figure 16-9 shows the output.

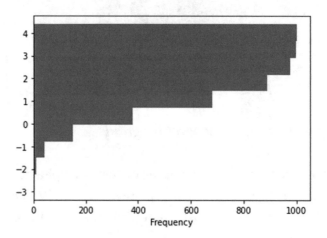

Figure 16-9. *Horizontal cumulative histogram*

The vertical version of the same histogram can be created as follows:

```
plt.figure();
df4['a'].plot.hist(orientation='vertical', cumulative=True)
plt.show()
```

Figure 16-10 shows the output.

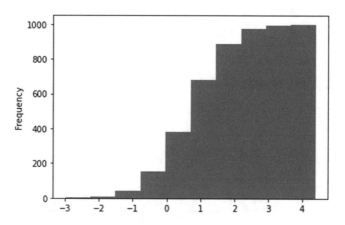

Figure 16-10. *Vertical cumulative histogram*

Let's try a fancy type of histogram next. The routine `diff()` computes the numeric difference between the previous row and the current one.

```
print(df4.diff())
```

The output will have the first row populated with NaN for all the columns (as there is no row before the first one). The output is as follows:

```
              a           b           c
0           NaN         NaN         NaN
1      0.431854    1.386333    0.882522
2     -1.845015   -2.827562   -0.823188
3      0.608762    2.417105    0.212552
4      1.034317   -0.530774    2.322213
..          ...         ...         ...
995    0.411207   -2.847858    0.325067
996   -0.310378    1.462998   -0.936370
997    1.814182   -0.171832    0.116622
998   -1.055230   -0.041384    0.579991
999   -2.465682    0.403880   -0.709485

[1000 rows x 3 columns]
```

Let's visualize this dataset, as shown here:

```
plt.figure()
df4.diff().hist(color='k', alpha=0.5, bins=50)
plt.show()
```

Figure 16-11 shows the output.

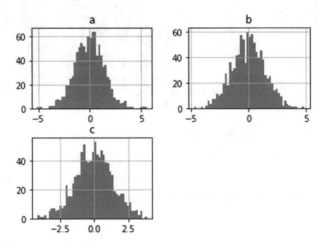

Figure 16-11. *Column-wise histograms*

You've just learned how to visualize datasets as histograms.

Box Plots

You can visualize data with box plots as well. Box plots (also spelled as *boxplots*) display the groups of numerical data through their quartiles. Let's create a dataset as follows:

```
df = pd.DataFrame(np.random.rand(10, 5),
                  columns=['A', 'B', 'C', 'D', 'E'])
print(df)
```

The generated dataset is as follows:

```
          A         B         C         D         E
0  0.684284  0.033906  0.099369  0.684024  0.533463
1  0.614305  0.645413  0.871788  0.561767  0.149080
2  0.226480  0.440091  0.096022  0.076962  0.674901
```

3	0.541253	0.409599	0.487924	0.649260	0.582250
4	0.436995	0.142239	0.781428	0.634987	0.825146
5	0.804633	0.874081	0.018661	0.306459	0.008134
6	0.228287	0.418942	0.157755	0.561070	0.740077
7	0.699860	0.230533	0.240369	0.108759	0.843307
8	0.530943	0.374583	0.650235	0.370809	0.595791
9	0.213455	0.221367	0.035203	0.887068	0.593629

You can draw box plots as follows:

```
plt.figure()
df.plot.box()
plt.show()
```

This will show the dataset as box plots, as shown in Figure 16-12.

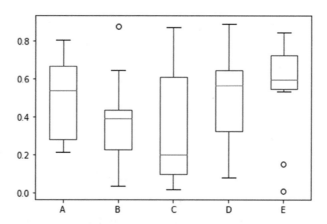

Figure 16-12. *Vertical box plot*

The colors shown here are the default values. You can change them. First, you need to create a dictionary as follows:

```
color = dict(boxes='DarkGreen',
             whiskers='DarkOrange',
             medians='DarkBlue',
             caps='Gray')
print(color)
```

The following is the output:

```
{'boxes': 'DarkGreen', 'whiskers': 'DarkOrange', 'medians': 'DarkBlue',
'caps': 'Gray'}
```

Finally, you pass this dictionary as an argument to the routine that draws the box plot as follows:

```
plt.figure()
df.plot.box(color=color, sym='r+')
plt.show()
```

Figure 16-13 shows the output.

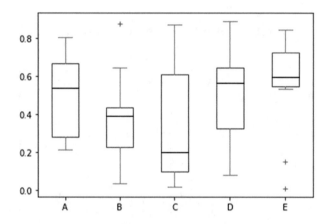

Figure 16-13. *Vertical box plot with customized colors*

The following example creates a horizontal box plot visualization:

```
plt.figure()
df.plot.box(vert=False, positions=[1, 2, 3, 4 , 5])
plt.show()
```

Figure 16-14 shows the output.

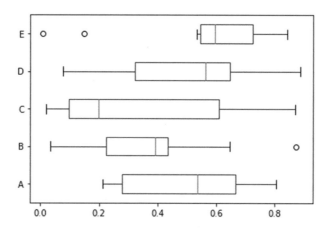

Figure 16-14. *Horizontal box plot*

Let's see another routine, boxplot(), that also creates box plots. For that, let's create another dataset, as shown here:

```
df = pd.DataFrame(np.random.rand(10, 5))
print(df)
```

The output dataset is as follows:

```
          0         1         2         3         4
0  0.936845  0.365561  0.890503  0.264896  0.937254
1  0.931661  0.226297  0.887385  0.036719  0.941609
2  0.127896  0.291034  0.161724  0.952966  0.925534
3  0.938686  0.336536  0.934843  0.806043  0.104054
4  0.743787  0.600116  0.989178  0.002870  0.453338
5  0.256692  0.773945  0.165381  0.809204  0.162431
6  0.822131  0.486780  0.453981  0.612403  0.614633
7  0.062387  0.958844  0.247515  0.573431  0.194665
8  0.453193  0.152337  0.062436  0.865115  0.220440
9  0.832040  0.237582  0.837805  0.423779  0.119027
```

You can draw box plots as follows:

```
plt.figure()
bp = df.boxplot()
plt.show()
```

Figure 16-15 shows the output.

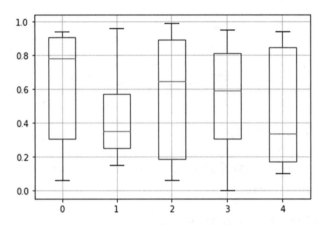

Figure 16-15. *Box plot in action*

The main advantage of the routine boxplot() is that you can have column-wise visualizations in a single output. Let's create an appropriate dataset as follows:

```
df = pd.DataFrame(np.random.rand(10, 2), columns=['Col1', 'Col2'] )
df['X'] = pd.Series(['A', 'A', 'A', 'A', 'A', 'B', 'B', 'B', 'B', 'B'])
print(df)
```

The output dataset is as follows:

```
        Col1        Col2   X
0   0.469416    0.341874   A
1   0.176359    0.921808   A
2   0.135188    0.149354   A
3   0.475295    0.360012   A
4   0.566289    0.142729   A
5   0.408705    0.571466   B
6   0.233820    0.470200   B
7   0.679833    0.633349   B
```

```
8   0.183652   0.559745   B
9   0.192431   0.726981   B
```

Let's create column-wise visualizations as follows:

```
plt.figure();
bp = df.boxplot(by='X')
plt.show()
```

The output will have a title by default explaining how the data is grouped, as shown in Figure 16-16.

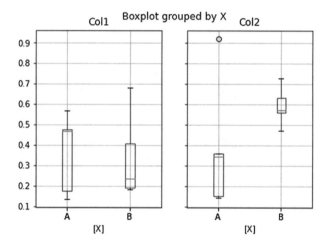

Figure 16-16.   *Box plots with groups*

Let's look at a little more complex example for this. The following is the code for a new dataset:

```
df = pd.DataFrame(np.random.rand(10,3), columns=['Col1', 'Col2', 'Col3'])
df['X'] = pd.Series(['A','A','A','A','A','B','B','B','B','B'])
df['Y'] = pd.Series(['A','B','A','B','A','B','A','B','A','B'])
print(df)
```

This code creates the following dataset:

```
      Col1       Col2       Col3   X   Y
0   0.542771   0.175804   0.017646   A
1   0.247552   0.503725   0.569475   A   B
```

2	0.593635	0.842846	0.755377	A
3	0.210409	0.235510	0.633318	A B
4	0.268419	0.170563	0.478912	A
5	0.526251	0.258278	0.549876	B
6	0.311182	0.212787	0.966183	B A
7	0.100687	0.432545	0.586907	B
8	0.416833	0.879384	0.635664	B A
9	0.249280	0.558648	0.661523	B

You can create box plots in groups of multiple columns (this means the grouping criteria will have multiple columns).

```
plt.figure();
bp = df.boxplot(column=['Col1','Col2'], by=['X','Y'])
plt.show()
```

Figure 16-17 shows the output.

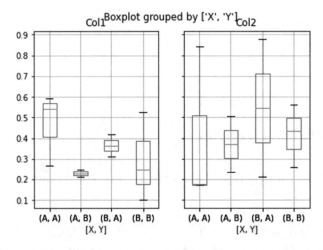

Figure 16-17. *Box plots with groups (multiple columns in the grouping criteria)*

Let's see a bit more complex example with a dataset that has more variation. The following code creates such a dataset:

```
np.random.seed(1234)
df_box = pd.DataFrame(np.random.randn(10, 2), columns=['A', 'B'])
```

```
df_box['C'] = np.random.choice(['Yes', 'No'], size=10)
print(df_box)
```

The output is the following dataset:

```
          A          B    C
0   0.471435  -1.190976   No
1   1.432707  -0.312652   Yes
2  -0.720589   0.887163   No
3   0.859588  -0.636524   Yes
4   0.015696  -2.242685   No
5   1.150036   0.991946   Yes
6   0.953324  -2.021255   No
7  -0.334077   0.002118   No
8   0.405453   0.289092   No
9   1.321158  -1.546906   No
```

You can use the routine groupby() in Pandas to group the data and visualize it as follows:

```
plt.figure()
bp = df_box.boxplot(by='C')
plt.show()
```

Figure 16-18 shows the output grouped by column C.

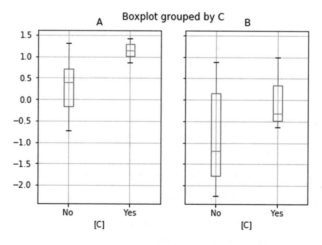

Figure 16-18.   *Box plot plt.figure()visualization grouped by column C*

Another example is as follows:

```
bp = df_box.groupby('C').boxplot()
plt.show()
```

Figure 16-19 shows the output.

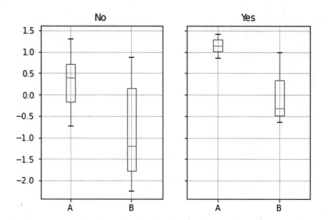

Figure 16-19. *Box plot visualization grouped by column C*

This is how you can visualize datasets as box plots.

Area Plots

You can visualize datasets as area plots too. Let's create a dataset with four columns as follows:

```
df = pd.DataFrame(np.random.rand(10, 4),
                  columns=['A', 'B', 'C', 'D'])
print(df)
```

This creates the following dataset:

```
          A          B          C          D
0   0.982005   0.123943   0.119381   0.738523
1   0.587304   0.471633   0.107127   0.229219
2   0.899965   0.416754   0.535852   0.006209
3   0.300642   0.436893   0.612149   0.918198
```

4	0.625737	0.705998	0.149834	0.746063
5	0.831007	0.633726	0.438310	0.152573
6	0.568410	0.528224	0.951429	0.480359
7	0.502560	0.536878	0.819202	0.057116
8	0.669422	0.767117	0.708115	0.796867
9	0.557761	0.965837	0.147157	0.029647

You can visualize all this data with the routine area() as follows:

```
plt.figure()
df.plot.area()
plt.show()
```

The previous example creates a stacked area plot, as shown in Figure 16-20.

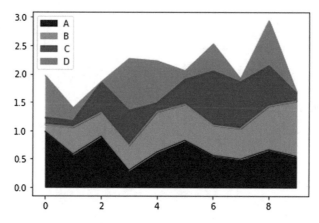

Figure 16-20. *Stacked area plots*

You can also create unstacked area plots by passing an argument to the routine area() as follows:

```
plt.figure()
df.plot.area(stacked=False)
plt.show()
```

The unstacked area plot will be transparent by default so that all the individual area plots are visible. Figure 16-21 shows the output.

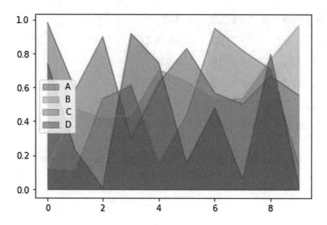

Figure 16-21. *Unstacked area plots*

This is how to create area plots.

Scatter Plots

You can also visualize any dataset as a scatter plot. Let's create a dataset as follows:

```
df = pd.DataFrame(np.random.rand(10, 4),
              columns=['A', 'B', 'C', 'D'])
print(df)
```

The output dataset is as follows:

```
          A         B         C         D
0   0.593893  0.114066  0.950810  0.325707
1   0.193619  0.457812  0.920403  0.879069
2   0.252616  0.348009  0.182589  0.901796
3   0.706528  0.726658  0.900088  0.779164
4   0.599155  0.291125  0.151395  0.335175
5   0.657552  0.073343  0.055006  0.323195
6   0.590482  0.853899  0.287062  0.173067
7   0.134021  0.994654  0.179498  0.317547
8   0.568291  0.009349  0.900649  0.977241
9   0.556895  0.084774  0.333002  0.728429
```

You can visualize columns A and B as a scatter plot as follows:

```
plt.figure()
df.plot.scatter(x='A', y='B')
plt.show()
```

Figure 16-22 shows the output.

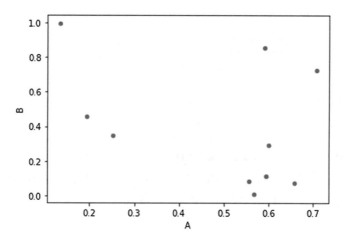

Figure 16-22. *Simple scatter plot*

You can visualize multiple groups as follows:

```
ax = df.plot.scatter(x='A', y='B',
                     color='Blue',
                     label='Group 1')
plt.figure()
df.plot.scatter(x='C', y='D',
                color='Green',
                label='Group 2',
                ax=ax)
plt.show()
```

Figure 16-23 shows the output.

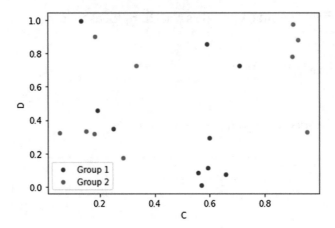

Figure 16-23. *Scatter plot with multiple groups*

Let's see how to customize the scatter plot. You can customize the color and the size of the points. The color or size can be a constant or can be variable. The following is an example of variable colors and a constant size for the data points. When the color is variable, a color bar is added to the output by default.

```
plt.figure()
df.plot.scatter(x='A', y='B', c='C', s=40)
plt.show()
```

Figure 16-24 shows the output.

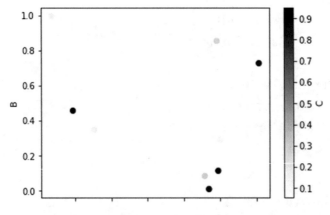

Figure 16-24. *Scatter plot with different colors for the data points*

Let's assign the size to be variable as follows:

```
plt.figure()
df.plot.scatter(x='A', y='B', s=df['C']*100)
plt.show()
```

Figure 16-25 shows the output.

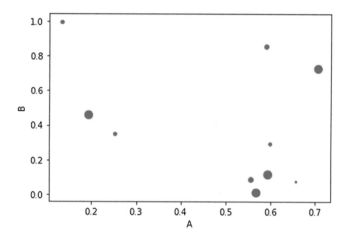

Figure 16-25. *Scatter plot with different sizes for the data points*

Finally, let's see an example with fully customized variable sizes and variable colors as follows:

```
plt.figure()
df.plot.scatter(x='A', y='B', c='C', s=df['D']*100)
plt.show()
```

Figure 16-26 shows the output.

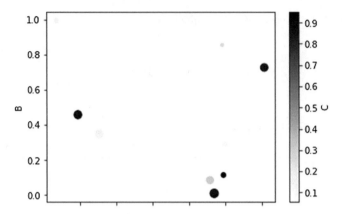

Figure 16-26. *Scatter plot with different sizes for the data points*

You've just learned how to create and customize scatter plots.

Hexagonal Bin Plots

You can also visualize data with hexagonal bin (hexbin) plots. Let's prepare a dataset as follows:

```
df = pd.DataFrame(np.random.randn(100, 2),
                  columns=['A', 'B'])
df['B'] = df['B'] + np.arange(100)
print(df)
```

The output is as follows:

```
          A          B
0    0.165445  -1.127470
1   -1.192185   1.818644
2    0.237185   1.663616
3    0.694727   3.750161
4    0.247055   4.645433
..       ...        ...
95   0.650346  94.485664
96   0.539429  97.526762
97  -3.277193  95.151439
```

```
98   0.672125   96.507021
99  -0.827198   99.914196
```

```
[100 rows x 2 columns]
```

Let's visualize this data with a hexbin plot as follows:

```
plt.figure()
df.plot.hexbin(x='A', y='B', gridsize=20)
plt.show()
```

Figure 16-27 shows the output.

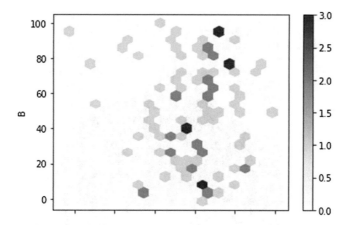

Figure 16-27. *Hexbin plot example*

As you can see, you can customize the size of the grid.

Pie Charts

Finally, you will learn how to create pie charts to visualize datasets. Let's create a dataset as follows:

```
series = pd.Series(3 * np.random.rand(4),
                   index=['A', 'B', 'C', 'D'],
                   name='series')
print(series)
```

This creates the following dataset:

```
A       1.566910
B       0.294986
C       2.140910
D       2.652122
Name: series, dtype: float64
```

You can visualize it as follows:

```
plt.figure()
series.plot.pie(figsize=(6, 6))
plt.show()
```

Figure 16-28 shows the output.

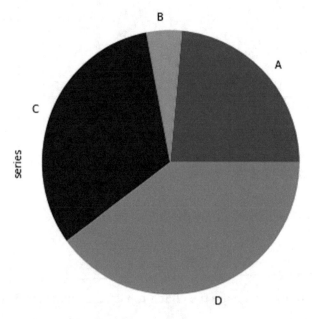

Figure 16-28. *A simple pie chart*

Let's create a dataset with two columns as follows:

```
df = pd.DataFrame(3 * np.random.rand(4, 2),
                  index=['A', 'B', 'C', 'D'],
                  columns=['X', 'Y'])
print(df)
```

This generates the following data:

```
        X           Y
A   1.701163   2.983445
B   0.536219   0.036600
C   1.370995   2.795256
D   2.538074   1.419990
```

Figure 16-29 shows the output.

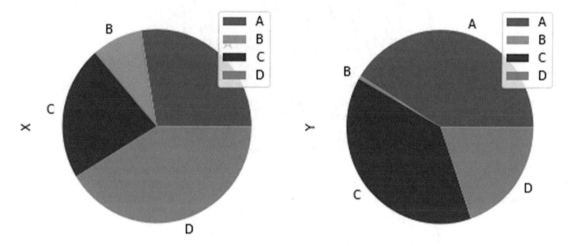

Figure 16-29. *A simple pie chart for a multicolumn dataset*

You can customize pie charts. Specifically, you can customize the font, colors, and labels as follows:

```
plt.figure()
series.plot.pie(labels=['A', 'B', 'C', 'D'],
                colors=['r', 'g', 'b', 'c'],
                autopct='%.2f', fontsize=20,
                figsize=(6, 6))
plt.show()
```

Figure 16-30 shows the output.

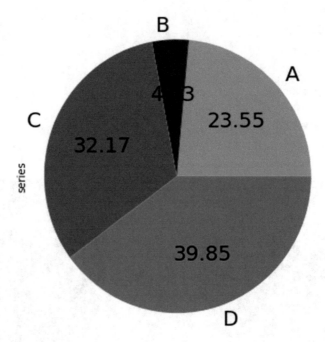

Figure 16-30. *A simple yet customized pie chart*

Let's create a partial pie chart by passing values whose sum is less than 1.0. The following is the data for that:

```
series = pd.Series([0.1] * 4,
                index=['A', 'B', 'C', 'D'],
                name='series2')
print(series)
```

This creates the following dataset:

```
A    0.1
B    0.1
C    0.1
D    0.1
Name: series2, dtype: float64
```

The partial pie chart can be visualized as follows:

```
plt.figure()
series.plot.pie(figsize=(6, 6))
plt.show()
```

This creates a partial pie chart (or a semicircle), as shown in Figure 16-31.

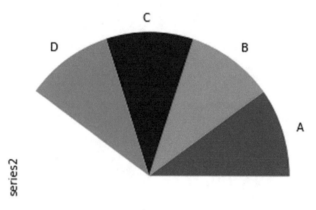

Figure 16-31. *A simple yet customized pie chart*

You've just learned how to visualize data with pie charts.

Summary

In this chapter, you learned how to visualize data with various techniques. You can use these visualization techniques in real-life projects. In the coming chapters, we will explore other libraries for creating data visualizations in Python.

In the next chapter, you will learn about how to create data visualizations with a new library called Seaborn.

CHAPTER 17

Introduction to Data Visualization with Seaborn

In the previous chapter, you learned how to visualize data stored in the Pandas series and dataframe.

In the previous chapters of this book, you studied the data visualization library Matplotlib extensively along with other important data science libraries called NumPy and Pandas. You will take a break in this chapter from Matplotlib and learn how to use another related library for data visualization called Seaborn. The following are the topics you will learn about in this chapter:

- What is Seaborn?

- Plotting statistical relationships

- Plotting lines

- Visualizing the distribution of data

After reading this chapter, you will be comfortable using the Seaborn library and will be able to create great visualizations of datasets.

What Is Seaborn?

You have learned how to use the Matplotlib library for data visualization. Matplotlib is not the only data visualization library in Python. There are numerous libraries in Python that can visualize data. The scientific data visualization libraries support the data structures of NumPy and Pandas. One such library for the visualization of scientific Python is Seaborn (`https://seaborn.pydata.org/index.html`). Seaborn is based on and built on top of Matplotlib. It provides a lot of functionality for drawing attractive

© Ashwin Pajankar 2022
A. Pajankar, *Hands-on Matplotlib*, https://doi.org/10.1007/978-1-4842-7410-1_17

graphics. It has built-in support for the series and dataframe data structures in Pandas and for Ndarrays in NumPy.

Let's create a new notebook for the demonstrations in this chapter. Now, let's install Seaborn with the following command:

```
!pip3 install seaborn
```

You can import the library to your notebook or a Python script with the following statement:

```
import seaborn as sns
```

You know that the Seaborn library supports the Pandas dataframes. The Seaborn library also has many dataframes stored in it that are populated with data. So, we can use them for our demonstrations. Let's see how to retrieve these dataframes. The following command returns the list of all the built-in sample dataframes:

```
sns.get_dataset_names()
```

The following is the output:

```
['anagrams',
 'anscombe',
 'attention',
 'brain_networks',
 'car_crashes',
 'diamonds',
 'dots',
 'exercise',
 'flights',
 'fmri',
 'gammas',
 'geyser',
 'iris',
 'mpg',
 'penguins',
 'planets',
 'tips',
 'titanic']
```

You can load these dataframes into Python variables as follows:

```
iris = sns.load_dataset('iris')
```

Let's see the data stored in the `iris` dataset with the following statement:

```
iris
```

Figure 17-1 shows the output.

```
In [6]: iris
```

Out[6]:	sepal_length	sepal_width	petal_length	petal_width	species
0	5.1	3.5	1.4	0.2	setosa
1	4.9	3.0	1.4	0.2	setosa
2	4.7	3.2	1.3	0.2	setosa
3	4.6	3.1	1.5	0.2	setosa
4	5.0	3.6	1.4	0.2	setosa
...	...	...	...	...	...
145	6.7	3.0	5.2	2.3	virginica
146	6.3	2.5	5.0	1.9	virginica
147	6.5	3.0	5.2	2.0	virginica
148	6.2	3.4	5.4	2.3	virginica
149	5.9	3.0	5.1	1.8	virginica

Figure 17-1. *The iris dataset*

Plotting Statistical Relationships

You can plot the statistical relationship between two variables with various functions in Seaborn. The general plotting function to do this is `relplot()`. You can plot various types of data with this function. By default, the `relplot()` function plots a scatter plot. Here is an example:

```
%matplotlib inline
import numpy as np
import pandas as pd
```

```
import matplotlib.pyplot as plt

sns.relplot(x='sepal_length',
            y='sepal_width',
            data=iris)
plt.grid('on')
plt.show()
```

This produces the scatter plot shown in Figure 17-2.

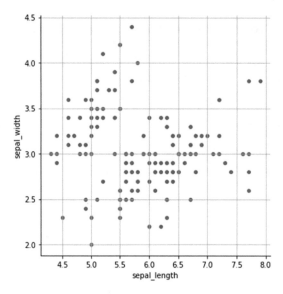

Figure 17-2. *The scatter plot*

You can explicitly specify the type of plot as follows:

```
sns.relplot(x='sepal_length', y='sepal_width',
            data=iris, kind='scatter')
plt.grid('on')
plt.show()
```

The function replot() is a generic function where you can pass an argument to specify the type of plot. You can also create a scatter plot with the function scatterplot(). For example, the following code creates the same result as shown in Figure 17-2:

```
sns.scatterplot(x='sepal_length',
                y='sepal_width',
                data=iris)
plt.grid('on')
plt.show()
```

You can feed some other columns of the dataset to the plotting function as follows:

```
sns.relplot(x='petal_length',
            y='petal_width',
            data=iris)
plt.grid('on')
plt.show()
```

Figure 17-3 shows the output.

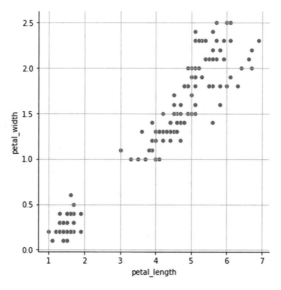

Figure 17-3. *Another example of a scatter plot*

You can also write this with the `scatterplot()` function as follows:

```
sns.scatterplot(x='petal_length',
                y='petal_width',
                data=iris)
plt.grid('on')
plt.show()
```

You can customize the plot and show an additional column with color coding as follows:

```
sns.relplot(x='sepal_length',
            y='sepal_width',
            hue='species',
            data=iris)
plt.grid('on')
plt.show()
```

Figure 17-4 shows the output.

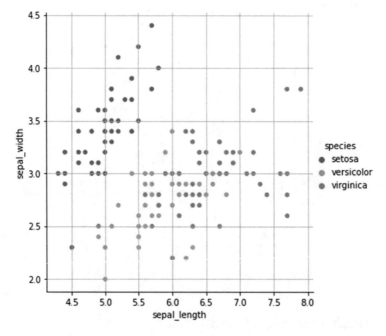

Figure 17-4. *Scatter plot with colors*

You get the same result as shown in Figure 17-4 with the following code:

```
sns.scatterplot(x='sepal_length',
                y='sepal_width',
                hue='species',
                data=iris)
plt.grid('on')
plt.show()
```

You can also assign the styles to the scatter plot data points (markers) as follows:

```
sns.relplot(x='sepal_length', y='sepal_width',
            hue='petal_length', style='species',
            data=iris)
plt.grid('on')
plt.show()
```

You can see the output in Figure 17-5.

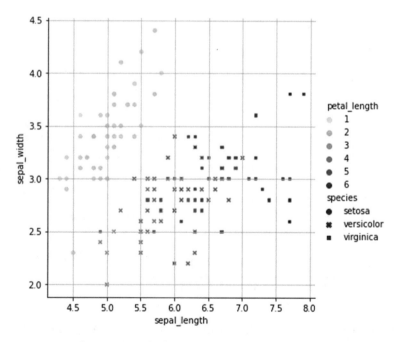

Figure 17-5. *Scatter plot with colors and custom styles*

The following code produces the same output as shown in Figure 17-5:

```
sns.scatterplot(x='sepal_length', y='sepal_width',
          hue='petal_length', style='species',
          data=iris)
plt.grid('on')
plt.show()
```

You can also adjust the sizes of the markers as follows:

```
sns.relplot(x='sepal_length', y='sepal_width',
          size='petal_length', style='species',
          hue='species', data=iris)
plt.grid('on')
plt.show()
```

Figure 17-6 shows the output.

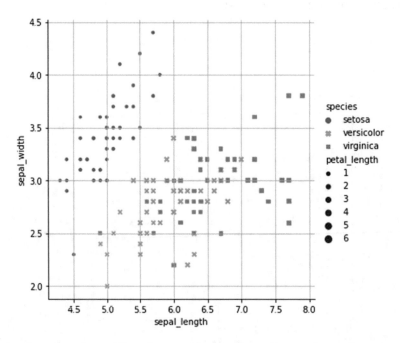

Figure 17-6. *Scatter plot with colors and custom styles and marker sizes*

The following code produces the same result as shown in Figure 17-5:

```
sns.scatterplot(x='sepal_length', y='sepal_width',
            size='petal_length', style='species',
            hue='species', data=iris)
plt.grid('on')
plt.show()
```

Plotting Lines

You can also show continuous data such as time-series data along a line. Time-series data has timestamp data in at least one column or has an index. A great example of a time series is a table of daily temperature records. Let's create a time-series dataframe to demonstrate the line plots.

```
df = pd.DataFrame(np.random.randn(100, 4),
                index=pd.date_range("1/1/2020",
                                    periods=100),
                columns=list("ABCD"))
df = df.cumsum()
```

You can use the function relplot() to draw the line as follows:

```
sns.relplot(x=df.index, y='A', kind="line", data=df)
plt.xticks(rotation=45)
plt.show()
```

Figure 17-7 shows the output.

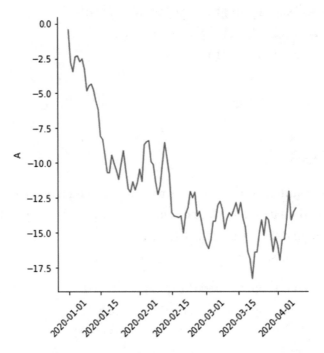

Figure 17-7. *Line plot of time-series data*

You can also produce the output shown in Figure 17-7 with the following code:

```
sns.lineplot(x=df.index,
             y='A', data=df)
plt.xticks(rotation=45)
plt.show()
```

In the next section, you will learn how to visualize the distribution of data.

Visualizing the Distribution of Data

One of the most prominent examples of visualizing the distribution of data is a frequency table or a frequency distribution table. You can create buckets of value ranges that the data can have (the domain), and then you can list the number of items that satisfy the criteria for the bucket. You can also vary the bucket size, with the smallest size being 1.

You can visually show the information of a frequency distribution using bars and lines. If you use bars, then it is known as a *histogram*. You can use the function `displot()` to visualize the frequency data. Let's start with dummy univariate data.

```
x = np.random.randn(100)
sns.displot(x)
plt.show()
```

Figure 17-8 shows the output.

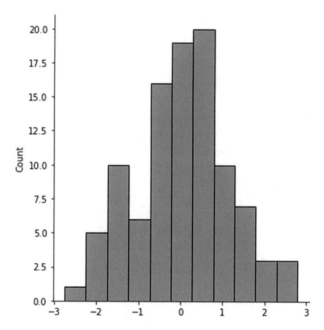

Figure 17-8. *Histogram*

You can also make it explicit that you need a histogram in the output as follows:

```
sns.displot(x, kind='hist')
plt.show()
```

A histogram is the default kind of graph. You can also show a Gaussian kernel density estimation (KDE) as follows:

```
sns.displot(x, kind='kde')
plt.show()
```

Figure 17-9 shows the output.

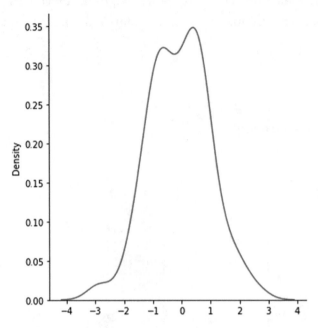

Figure 17-9. *KDE graph*

You can visualize an empirical cumulative distribution function (eCDF) as follows:

```
sns.displot(x, kind='ecdf')
plt.show()
```

Figure 17-10 shows the output.

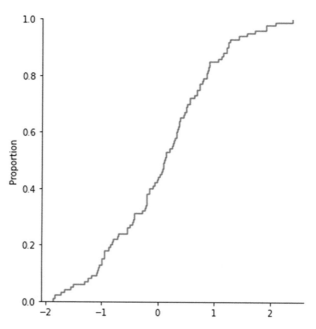

Figure 17-10. *eCDF graph*

You can combine a histogram and a KDE as follows:

```
sns.displot(x, kind='hist', kde=True)
plt.show()
```

Figure 17-11 shows the output.

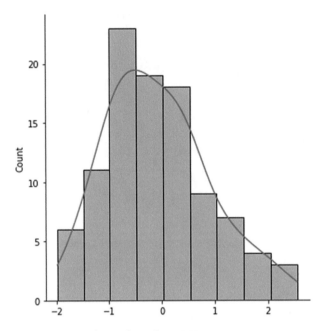

Figure 17-11. *Histogram combined with KDE*

Now let's use some real-life data, as follows:

```
tips = sns.load_dataset("tips")
sns.displot(x='total_bill', data=tips, kind='hist')
plt.show()
```

Figure 17-12 shows the output.

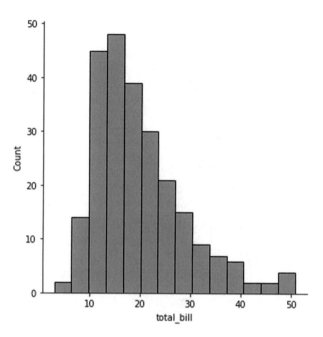

Figure 17-12. *Real-life data visualized as a histogram*

You can customize the size of bins (or buckets) in the visualization as follows:

```
sns.displot(x='total_bill', data=tips,
          kind='hist', bins=30, kde=True)
plt.show()
```

Figure 17-13 shows the output.

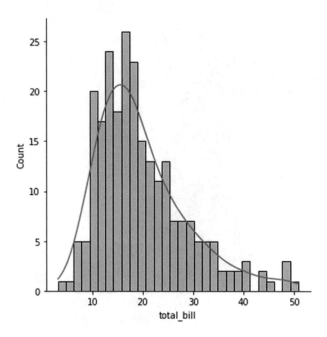

Figure 17-13. *Customized buckets in a histogram*

You can adjust the hue of the plots based on a criterion of your choice as follows:

```
sns.displot(x='total_bill', data=tips,
            kind='kde', hue='size')
plt.show()
```

Figure 17-14 shows the output.

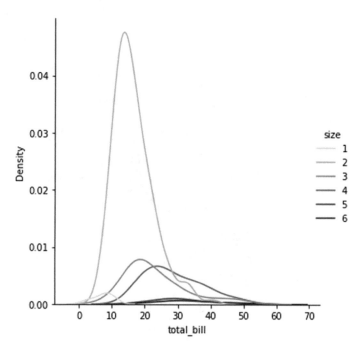

Figure 17-14. *Customized colors in a KDE plot*

Up to now, we have used a single variable to show the plot. When you use two variables for plotting, it is known as a *bivariate* plot. Here is a simple example:

```
sns.displot(x='total_bill',
            y='tip', data=tips)
plt.show()
```

Figure 17-15 shows the output.

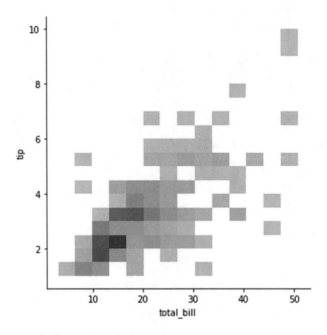

Figure 17-15. *A simple bivariate histogram*

You can add color to this example as follows:

```
sns.displot(x='total_bill', y='tip',
            hue='size', data=tips)
plt.show()
```

Figure 17-16 shows the output.

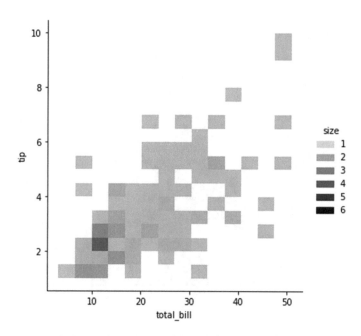

Figure 17-16. *A simple bivariate histogram with color*

You can also customize the size of bins and add ticks on the x- and y-axes (known as a *rug plot*) as follows:

```
sns.displot(x='total_bill', y='tip',
          data=tips, rug=True,
          kind='hist', bins=30)
plt.show()
```

Figure 17-17 shows the output.

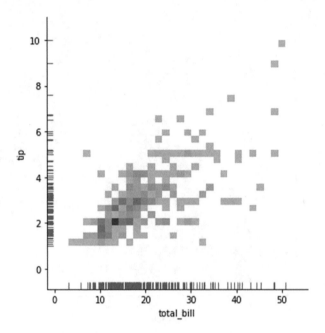

Figure 17-17. *A simple bivariate histogram with custom bins and rug plot*

A more interesting type of visualization is a bivariate KDE plot. It looks like a contour. The code is as follows:

```
sns.displot(x='total_bill', y='tip',
          data=tips, kind='kde')
plt.show()
```

Figure 17-18 shows the output.

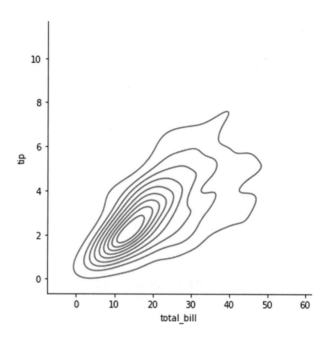

Figure 17-18. *A simple bivariate KDE plot*

You can add a rug plot to the output as follows:

```
sns.displot(x='total_bill', y='tip',
            data=tips, rug=True,
            kind='kde')
plt.show()
```

The output has KDE and rug visualizations, both as shown in Figure 17-19.

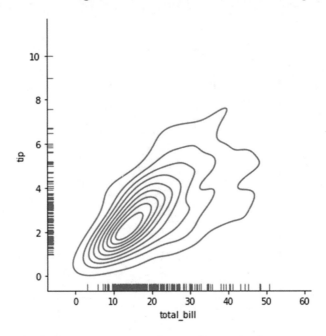

Figure 17-19. *A simple bivariate KDE plot with a rug plot*

Based on the columns in the dataframe, you can create individual visualizations arranged in rows or columns. Let's create a visualization based on the size of tips as follows:

```
sns.displot(x='total_bill', y='tip',
          data=tips, rug=True,
          kind='kde', col='size')
plt.show()
```

In the previous example, we are enabling the rug plot feature, and the plots will be separately generated based on the sizes of the tips. Figure 17-20 shows the output.

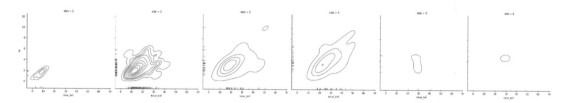

Figure 17-20. *A simple bivariate KDE plot with a rug plot arranged in columns*

You can also arrange the individual graphs in rows as follows:

```
sns.displot(x='total_bill', y='tip',
          data=tips, rug=True,
          kind='kde', row='size')
plt.show()
```

Figure 17-21 shows the output.

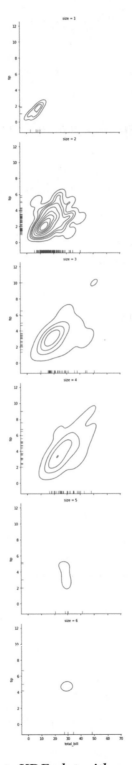

Figure 17-21. *A simple bivariate KDE plot with a rug plot arranged in rows*

You've just learned how to visualize the distribution of data.

Summary

This chapter contained lots of demonstrations. You explored the Seaborn data visualization library of Python in detail. Seaborn is a vast library, and we have just scratched its surface in this chapter. You can refer to the home page of the Seaborn project at `https://seaborn.pydata.org/index.html` for the API documentation, tutorials, and an example gallery.

In the next and final chapter of this book, you will learn how to visualize the real-life data of the currently ongoing COVID-19 pandemic with the Matplotlib and Seaborn data visualization libraries.

CHAPTER 18

Visualizing Real-Life Data with Matplotlib and Seaborn

In the previous chapter, you learned how to visualize data with a new data visualization library for scientific Python tasks. You learned to create visualizations from data stored in various formats.

In this chapter, you will take all the knowledge you have obtained in the earlier chapters of this book and put it together to prepare visualizations for real-life data from the COVID-19 pandemic and animal disease datasets obtained from the Internet. The following are the topics you will explore in this chapter:

- COVID-19 pandemic data

- Fetching the pandemic data programmatically

- Preparing the data for visualization

- Creating visualizations with Matplotlib and Seaborn

- Creating visualizations of animal disease data

After reading this chapter, you will be comfortable working with and creating visualizations of real-life datasets.

COVID-19 Pandemic Data

The world is facing the COVID-19 pandemic as of this writing (May 2021). COVID-19 is caused by severe acute respiratory syndrome coronavirus 2 (SARS-CoV-2). The symptoms include common flu-like symptoms and breathing troubles.

© Ashwin Pajankar 2022
A. Pajankar, *Hands-on Matplotlib*, https://doi.org/10.1007/978-1-4842-7410-1_18

There are multiple organizations in the world that collect and share real-time data for pandemics. One is Johns Hopkins University (`https://coronavirus.jhu.edu/map.html`), and the other one is Worldometers (`https://www.worldometers.info/coronavirus/`). Both of these web pages have data about the COVID-19 pandemic, and they are refreshed quite frequently. Figure 18-1 shows the Johns Hopkins page for COVID-19.

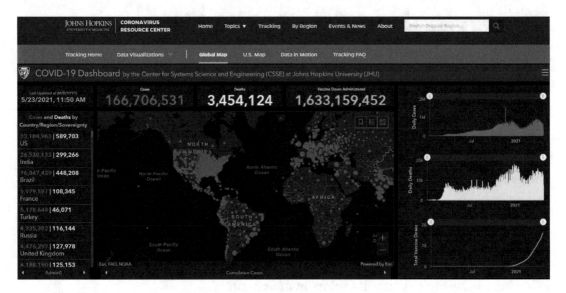

Figure 18-1. *Johns Hopkins COVID-19 home page*

Figure 18-2 shows the Worldometers website.

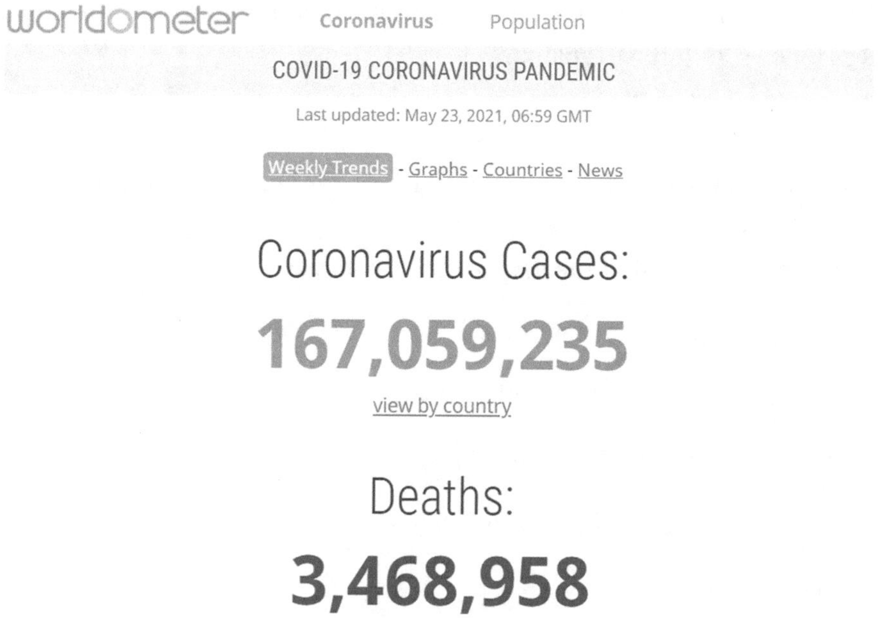

worldometer   **Coronavirus**   Population

COVID-19 CORONAVIRUS PANDEMIC

Last updated: May 23, 2021, 06:59 GMT

Weekly Trends - Graphs - Countries - News

Coronavirus Cases:

167,059,235

view by country

Deaths:

3,468,958

Figure 18-2. *Worldometers COVID-19 home page*

As I mentioned, the data is refreshed on a frequent basis, so these websites are quite reliable for up-to-date information.

Fetching the Pandemic Data Programmatically

In this section, you will learn how to fetch both datasets (Johns Hopkins and Worldometers) using Python programs. To do that, you need to install a library for Python. The library's home page is located at `https://ahmednafies.github.io/covid/`, and the PyPI page is `https://pypi.org/project/covid/`. Create a new notebook for this chapter using Jupyter Notebook. You can easily install the library with the following command in the notebook:

```
!pip3 install covid
```

You can import the library to a notebook or a Python script/program as follows:

```
from covid import Covid
```

You can create an object to fetch the data from an online source. By default, the data source is as follows for Johns Hopkins:

```
covid = Covid()
```

Note that due to high traffic, sometimes the servers are unresponsive. I experienced this multiple times.

You can explicitly mention the data source as follows:

```
covid = Covid(source="john_hopkins")
```

You can specify Worldometers explicitly as follows:

```
covid = Covid(source="worldometers")
```

You can see the source of the data as follows:

```
covid.source
```

Based on the data source, this returns a relevant string, as shown here:

```
'john_hopkins'
```

You can get status by country name as follows:

```
covid.get_status_by_country_name("italy")
```

This returns a dictionary, as follows:

```
{'id': '86',
 'country': 'Italy',
 'confirmed': 4188190,
 'active': 283744,
 'deaths': 125153,
 'recovered': 3779293,
 'latitude': 41.8719,
 'longitude': 12.5674,
 'last_update': 1621758045000}
```

You can also fetch the status by country ID, although only the Johns Hopkins dataset has this column, so the code will return an error for Worldometers.

```
# Only valid for Johns Hopkins
covid.get_status_by_country_id(115)
```

The output is similar to the earlier example, as shown here:

```
{'id': '115',
 'country': 'Mexico',
 'confirmed': 2395330,
 'active': 261043,
 'deaths': 221597,
 'recovered': 1912690,
 'latitude': 23.6345,
 'longitude': -102.5528,
 'last_update': 1621758045000}
```

You can also fetch the list of countries as follows:

```
covid.list_countries()
```

Here is part of the output:

```
[{'id': '179', 'name': 'US'},
 {'id': '80', 'name': 'India'},
 {'id': '24', 'name': 'Brazil'},
 {'id': '63', 'name': 'France'},
 {'id': '178', 'name': 'Turkey'},
 {'id': '143', 'name': 'Russia'},
 {'id': '183', 'name': 'United Kingdom'},
....
```

You will continue using the Johns Hopkins dataset throughout the chapter.

You can get active cases as follows:

```
covid.get_total_active_cases()
```

The output is as follows:

```
27292520
```

You can get the total confirmed cases as follows:

```
covid.get_total_confirmed_cases()
```

The output is as follows:

```
166723247
```

You can get the total recovered cases as follows:

```
covid.get_total_recovered()
```

The output is as follows:

```
103133392
```

You can get total deaths as follows:

```
covid.get_total_deaths()
```

The output is as follows:

```
3454602
```

You can fetch all the data with the function call covid.get_data(). This returns a list of dictionaries where every dictionary holds the data of one country. The following is the output:

```
[{'id': '179',
  'country': 'US',
  'confirmed': 33104963,
  'active': None,
  'deaths': 589703,
  'recovered': None,
  'latitude': 40.0,
  'longitude': -100.0,
  'last_update': 1621758045000},
 {'id': '80',
  'country': 'India',
  'confirmed': 26530132,
  'active': 2805399,
  'deaths': 299266,
```

```
'recovered': 23425467,
'latitude': 20.593684,
'longitude': 78.96288,
'last_update': 1621758045000},
......
```

Preparing the Data for Visualization

You have to prepare this fetched data for visualization. For that you have to convert the list of dictionaries in the Pandas dataframe. It can be done as follows:

```
import pandas as pd
df = pd.DataFrame(covid.get_data())
print(df)
```

Figure 18-3 shows the output.

```
          id          country  confirmed      active  deaths    recovered  \
0        179               US   33104963         NaN  589703          NaN
1         80            India   26530132   2805399.0  299266   23425467.0
2         24           Brazil   16047439   1466788.0  448208   14132443.0
3         63           France    5979597   5161260.0  108345     382519.0
4        178           Turkey    5178648    119466.0   46071    5013111.0
..       ...              ...        ...         ...     ...          ...
187      105       MS Zaandam          9         0.0       2          7.0
188      112  Marshall Islands          4         0.0       0          4.0
189      186          Vanuatu          4         0.0       1          3.0
190      148            Samoa          3         0.0       0          3.0
191      116        Micronesia          1         0.0       0          1.0

      latitude   longitude    last_update
0    40.000000  -100.00000  1621758045000
1    20.593684    78.96288  1621758045000
2   -14.235000   -51.92530  1621758045000
3    46.227600     2.21370  1621758045000
4    38.963700    35.24330  1621758045000
..         ...         ...            ...
```

Figure 18-3. *Pandas dataframe for COVID-19 data*

You can sort it as follows:

```
sorted = df.sort_values(by=['confirmed'], ascending=False)
```

Then you have to exclude the data for the world and continents so only the data for the individual countries remains.

```
excluded = sorted [ ~sorted.country.isin(['Europe', 'Asia',
                                          'South America',
                                          'World', 'Africa',
                                          'North America'])]
```

Let's find out the top ten records.

```
top10 = excluded.head(10)
print(top10)
```

You can then assign the columns to the individual variables as follows:

```
x = top10.country
y1 = top10.confirmed
y2 = top10.active
y3 = top10.deaths
y4 = top10.recovered
```

Creating Visualizations with Matplotlib and Seaborn

Let's visualize the data with Matplotlib and Seaborn. First import all the needed libraries, as shown here:

```
%matplotlib inline
import matplotlib.pyplot as plt
import seaborn as sns
```

A simple linear plot can be obtained as follows:

```
plt.plot(x, y1)
plt.xticks(rotation=90)
plt.show()
```

Figure 18-4 shows the output.

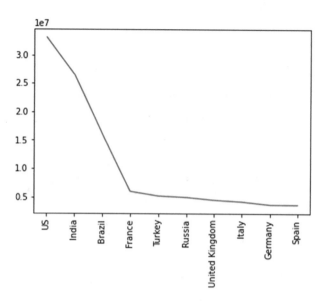

Figure 18-4. *Linear plot with Matplotlib*

You can add a title to this plot. You can also use the Seaborn library for it. The following is an example of a line plot with Seaborn:

```
sns.set_theme(style='whitegrid')
sns.lineplot(x=x, y=y1)
plt.xticks(rotation=90)
plt.show()
```

In the code example, we are using the function set_theme(). It sets the theme for the entire notebook for the Matplotlib and Seaborn visualizations. You can pass one of the strings 'darkgrid', 'whitegrid', 'dark', 'white', or 'ticks' as an argument to this function. Figure 18-5 shows the output.

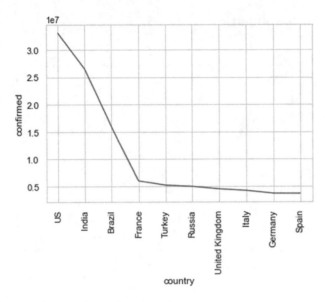

Figure 18-5. *Linear plot with Seaborn*

You can create a simple bar plot with Matplotlib as follows:

```
plt.bar(x, y1)
plt.xticks(rotation=45)
plt.show()
```

Figure 18-6 shows the output.

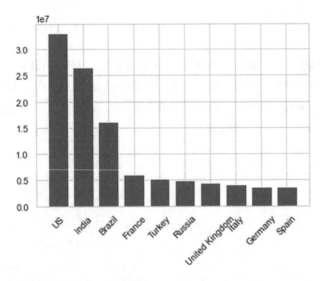

Figure 18-6. *Bar plot with Matplotlib*

The same visualization can be prepared with Seaborn, which produces a much better bar plot aesthetically.

```
sns.barplot(x=x, y=y1)
plt.xticks(rotation=45)
plt.show()
```

Figure 18-7 shows the output.

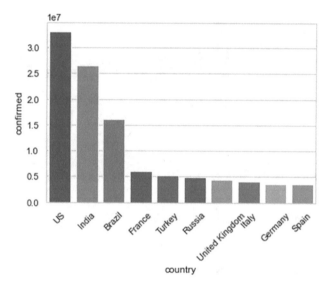

Figure 18-7. *Bar plot with Seaborn*

You can even change the color palette as follows:

```
sns.barplot(x=x, y=y1,
            palette="Blues_d")
plt.xticks(rotation=45)
plt.show()
```

Figure 18-8 shows the output.

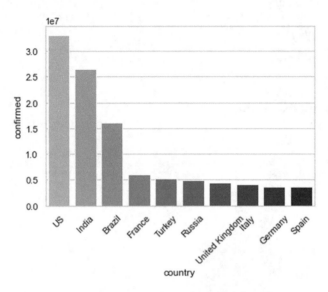

Figure 18-8. *Bar plot using Seaborn with custom palette*

You can create a multiline graph as follows:

```
labels = ['Confirmed', 'Active', 'Deaths', 'Recovered']
plt.plot(x, y1, x, y2, x, y3, x, y4)
plt.legend(labels, loc='upper right')
plt.xticks(rotation=90)
plt.show()
```

Figure 18-9 shows the output.

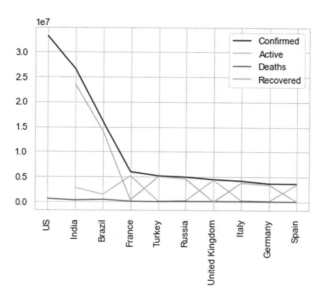

Figure 18-9. *Multiline graph*

You can use the Seaborn library to create the same graph as follows:

```
sns.lineplot(x=x, y=y1)
sns.lineplot(x=x, y=y2)
sns.lineplot(x=x, y=y3)
sns.lineplot(x=x, y=y4)
plt.legend(labels, loc='upper right')
plt.xticks(rotation=45)
plt.show()
```

Figure 18-10 shows the output.

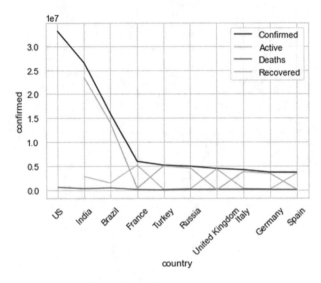

Figure 18-10. *Multiline graph with Seaborn*

You will now see how to create a multiple-bar graph with Matplotlib as follows:

```
df2 = pd.DataFrame([y1, y2, y3, y4])
df2.plot.bar()
plt.legend(x, loc='best')
plt.xticks(rotation=45)
plt.show()
```

Figure 18-11 shows the output.

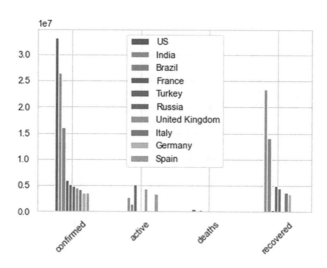

Figure 18-11. *Multiline bar graph*

You can even show this in a horizontal fashion as follows:

```
df2.plot.barh()
plt.legend(x, loc='best')
plt.xticks(rotation=45)
plt.show()
```

Figure 18-12 shows the output.

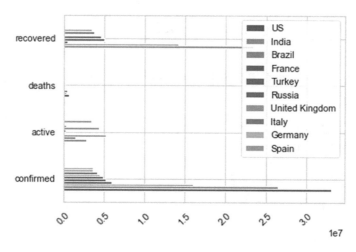

Figure 18-12. *Multiline horizontal graph*

You can use Seaborn to create a scatter plot as follows:

```
sns.scatterplot(x=x, y=y1)
sns.scatterplot(x=x, y=y2)
sns.scatterplot(x=x, y=y3)
sns.scatterplot(x=x, y=y4)
plt.legend(labels, loc='best')
plt.xticks(rotation=45)
plt.show()
```

Figure 18-13 shows the output.

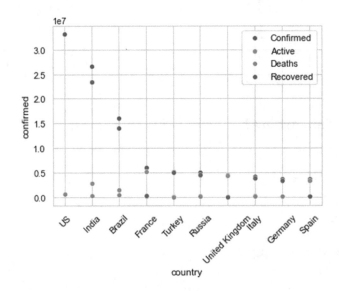

Figure 18-13. *Multiline horizontal bar graph*

You can even create an area plot with Matplotlib with the following code:

```
df2.plot.area()
plt.legend(x, loc='best')
plt.xticks(rotation=45)
plt.show()
```

Figure 18-14 shows the output.

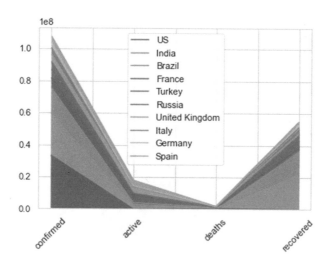

Figure 18-14. *Stacked area plot*

You can create an unstacked and transparent area plot for the data as follows:

```
df2.plot.area(stacked=False)
plt.legend(x, loc='best')
plt.xticks(rotation=45)
plt.show()
```

Figure 18-15 shows the output.

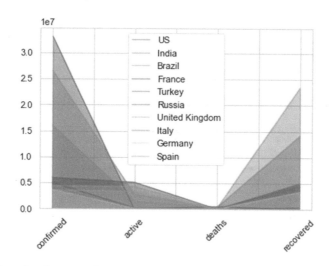

Figure 18-15. *Stacked area plot*

You can create a pie chart as follows:

```
plt.pie(y3, labels=x)
plt.title('Death Toll')
plt.show()
```

Figure 18-16 shows the output.

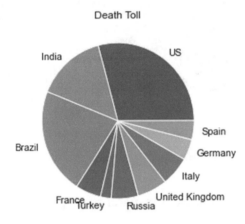

Figure 18-16. *Pie chart*

You can also create a KDE plot with a rug plot, but with the data that we're using for this example, that may not make a lot of sense.

```
sns.set_theme(style="ticks")
sns.kdeplot(x=y1)
sns.rugplot(x=y1)
plt.show()
```

Figure 18-17 shows the output.

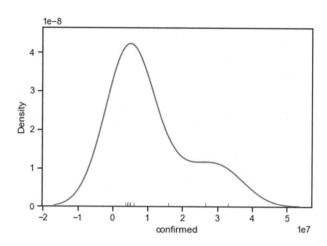

Figure 18-17. KDE plot

Creating Visualizations of Animal Disease Data

You can create visualizations for other real-life datasets too. Let's create visualizations for animal disease data. Let's first read it from an online repository.

```
df = pd.read_csv("https://github.com/Kesterchia/Global-animal-diseases/
blob/main/Data/Outbreak_240817.csv?raw=True")
```

Let's see the top five records.

```
df.head()
```

Figure 18-18 shows the output.

Out[36]:

	Id	source	latitude	longitude	region	country	admin1	localityName
0	230399	OIE	-27.900000	30.800000	Africa	South Africa	KwaZulu-Natal	HPAI_H5N8_2017_019
1	230381	OIE	54.837037	73.354155	Europe	Russian Federation	Omskaya Oblast	Novaya Stanica
2	230333	OIE	-21.077740	30.211620	Africa	Zimbabwe	Masvingo	Mwambe
3	230396	OIE	-26.000000	28.300000	Africa	South Africa	Gauteng	HPAI_H5N8_2017_020
4	230371	OIE	49.237900	17.700200	Europe	Czech Republic	Jihomoravsky	Hvozdná

5 rows × 24 columns

Figure 18-18. *Animal disease data*

Let's get information about the columns as follows:

```
df.info()
```

The output is as follows:

```
<class 'pandas.core.frame.DataFrame'>
RangeIndex: 17008 entries, 0 to 17007
Data columns (total 24 columns):
 #   Column            Non-Null Count   Dtype
---  ------            --------------   -----
 0   Id                17008 non-null   int64
 1   source            17008 non-null   object
 2   latitude          17008 non-null   float64
 3   longitude         17008 non-null   float64
 4   region            17008 non-null   object
 5   country           17008 non-null   object
 6   admin1            17008 non-null   object
 7   localityName      17008 non-null   object
 8   localityQuality   17008 non-null   object
 9   observationDate   16506 non-null   object
 10  reportingDate     17008 non-null   object
 11  status            17008 non-null   object
```

```
12   disease            17008 non-null   object
13   serotypes          10067 non-null   object
14   speciesDescription 15360 non-null   object
15   sumAtRisk           9757 non-null   float64
16   sumCases           14535 non-null   float64
17   sumDeaths          14168 non-null   float64
18   sumDestroyed       13005 non-null   float64
19   sumSlaughtered     12235 non-null   float64
20   humansGenderDesc    360 non-null    object
21   humansAge          1068 non-null    float64
22   humansAffected     1417 non-null    float64
23   humansDeaths        451 non-null    float64
dtypes: float64(10), int64(1), object(13)
memory usage: 3.1+ MB
```

Let's perform a "group by" operation on the column country and compute the sum of total cases, as shown here:

```
df2 = pd.DataFrame(df.groupby('country').sum('sumCases')['sumCases'])
```

Now let's sort and select the top ten cases.

```
df3 = df2.sort_values(by='sumCases', ascending = False).head(10)
```

Let's plot a bar graph, using the following code:

```
df3.plot.bar()
plt.xticks(rotation=90)
plt.show()
```

Figure 18-19 shows the output.

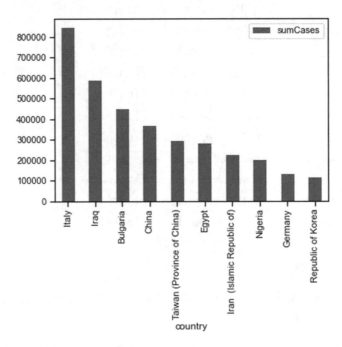

Figure 18-19. *Bar chart*

You can convert the index to a column as follows:

```
df3.reset_index(level=0, inplace=True)
df3
```

The output is as follows:

	country	sumCases
0	Italy	846756.0
1	Iraq	590049.0
2	Bulgaria	453353.0
3	China	370357.0
4	Taiwan (Province of China)	296268.0
5	Egypt	284449.0
6	Iran (Islamic Republic of)	225798.0
7	Nigeria	203688.0
8	Germany	133425.0
9	Republic of Korea	117018.0

Let's make a pie chart as follows:

```
plt.pie(df3['sumCases'],
        labels=df3['country'])
plt.title('Death Toll')
plt.show()
```

Figure 18-20 shows the output.

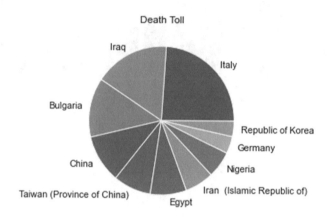

Figure 18-20. *Pie chart*

You can create a more aesthetically pleasing bar chart with Seaborn as follows:

```
sns.barplot(x='country',
            y='sumCases',
            data=df3)
plt.xticks(rotation=90)
plt.show()
```

Figure 18-21 shows the output.

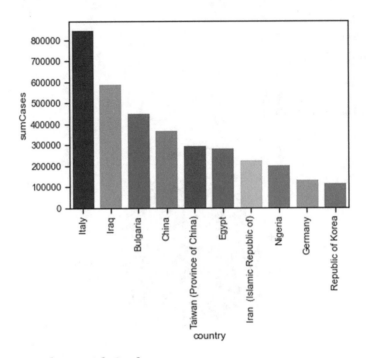

Figure 18-21. *Bar chart with Seaborn*

You've just learned to visualize real-life animal disease data.

Summary

In this chapter, you explored more functionality of the Seaborn data visualization library, which is part of the scientific Python ecosystem. You also learned how to import real-life data into Jupyter Notebook. You used the Matplotlib and Seaborn libraries to visualize the data.

As you know, this is the last chapter in the book. While we explored Matplotlib in great detail, we have just scratched the surface of the vast body of knowledge and programming APIs. You now have the knowledge to further explore Matplotlib and other data visualization libraries on your own. Python has many data visualization libraries for scientific data. Examples include Plotly, Altair, and Cartopy. Armed with your knowledge of the basics of data visualization, have fun continuing your journey further into data science and visualization!

Index

© Ashwin Pajankar 2022
A. Pajankar, *Hands-on Matplotlib*, https://doi.org/10.1007/978-1-4842-7410-1

Printed in the United States
by Baker & Taylor Publisher Services